The Trinitarian Self

Princeton Theological Monograph Series

K. C. Hanson, Charles M. Collier, and
D. Christopher Spinks, Series Editors

Recent volumes in the series

Kevin Twain Lowery
Salvaging Wesley's Agenda: A New Paradigm for Wesleyan Virtue Ethics

D. Seiple and Frederick W. Weidmann, editors
Enigmas and Powers: Engaging the Work of Walter Wink for Classroom, Church, and World

Stanley D. Walters
Go Figure!: Figuration in Biblical Interpretation

Paul S. Chung
Martin Luther and Buddhism: Aesthetics of Suffering, Second Edition

Steven B. Sherman
Revitalizing Theological Epistemology: Holistic Evangelical Approaches to the Knowledge of God

Mary Clark Moschella
Living Devotions: Reflections on Immigration, Identity, and Religious Imagination

Michael S. Hogue
The Tangled Bank: Toward an Ecotheolgical Ethics of Responsible Participation

Abraham Varghese Kunnuthara
Schleiermacher on Christian Consciousness of God's Work in History

Christian T. Collins Winn
"Jesus is Victor!": The Significance of the Blumhardts for the Theology of Karl Barth

The Trinitarian Self

The Key to the Puzzle of Violence

Charles K. Bellinger

PICKWICK *Publications* • Eugene, Oregon

THE TRINITARIAN SELF
The Key to the Puzzle of Violence

Princeton Theological Monograph Series 88

www.wipfandstock.com

ISBN 13: 978-1-55635-232-4

Cataloging-in-Publication data:

Bellinger, Charles K., 1962–

The trinitarian self : the key to the puzzle of violence / Charles K. Bellinger.

xxii + 192 p.; 23 cm. — Princeton Theological Monograph Series 88

Includes bibliographical references and index.

ISBN 13: 978-1-55635-232-4

1. Kierkegaard, Søren, 1813–1855. 2. Voegelin, Eric, 1901–1985. 3. Girard, René, 1923–. 4. Violence—Religious aspects—Christianity. 5. Christian ethics. 6. Trinity. 7. Theological anthropology—Christianity. I. Title. II. Series.

BT736.15 .B47 2008

Manufactured in the U.S.A.

For Daisy and Luke

Contents

Charts

Preface

THE JULY 24, 2006 ISSUE OF *TIME MAGAZINE* FEATURED THIS COVER headline: "Why They Fight, And Why It's Different This Time." They were referring to an outbreak of violence between the Israeli army and Hezbollah militants. As I read the articles, however, two thoughts ran through my head: (1) why human beings fight is not actually being explained, and (2) it isn't different this time; this is another example of the same reciprocal violence that has plagued the Middle East for decades.

Why human beings are violent is not a question that is asked very often in the journalistic world, at least not in a way that has substance and depth. I do not mean to pick on journalists; they are simply representatives of society in general. We human beings are not usually interested in asking why we human beings are violent. The question is too emotionally charged and dangerous to be asked. Notice the way the *Time* headline was worded: "Why *They* Fight." If it had read "Why *We* Fight," with the *we* understood as referring to the whole human race, then the paradigm of thought would have shifted dramatically, but such a shift is not on the agenda of journalists or politicians or military leaders or educators or religious leaders. (This blanket statement is generally true, although there are a few exceptions.) Hunger to understand violence at a deep level is simply not a part of normal everyday discourse, or of our educational system that produces the discourse. Both the journalists and the public for which they write manifest a lack of curiosity, which in less mild terms can be described as intellectual sloth and apathy.

Developing a psychological comprehension of violent behavior is an ethical imperative in our age. The luxury of ignorance is no longer possible. It is not acceptable for people to think that developing such a comprehension is the task only of social scientists. We all must become social scientists to a certain degree by reflecting on the roots of violence. If we refuse to do so we are resisting our ethical calling. To express this idea more sharply: if we do not strive to understand violence, we are supporting the atmosphere of ignorance from which violence draws its energy, like a hurricane draws energy from warm water.

This book presents a paradigm for understanding human violence. That is its central argument and purpose. I suggest that if we do develop a deep comprehension of the psychological roots of violence, and spread this comprehension throughout society through education, then we will be accomplishing something of immense historical significance. We will be bringing about what can be called a New Copernican Revolution. For the human race to move from not understanding its own violence to understanding it is not only similar to the first Copernican Revolution, which gave us an accurate conception of the solar system, but it is in fact of much greater importance than that first revolution. Modern science has given us an understanding of the external world of physical things, but understanding our internal, psychological world as human beings is much more important in the long run.

The problem, however, is that to understand the roots of violence is not simply another piece of knowledge, like learning how a frog develops from a tadpole or how an internal combustion engine works. This understanding requires changes in the knower that make the reception of the knowledge possible. Unlike many other forms of knowledge, this comprehension can come to fruition only in the wake of a spiritual and intellectual conversion. This explains why this form of understanding is so rare in our world (because real conversion is rare), and it explains why there is not simply a lack of interest in developing an understanding of violence, but actually resistance to it.

The paradigm for comprehending violence that is articulated in this book takes the form of an anthropology that uses theological ideas to interpret specific observable behaviors. I am suggesting that theological anthropology could actually compete with "secular social science" in the task of making sense of the actions of Hitler, Stalin, and the 9/11 hijackers. I argue that while it may be difficult for there to be a theological mathematics or chemistry, there most certainly can and ought to be a theological political science and psychology. Such a science is not simply a possibility; I argue that it is already an actuality if we have eyes to see it. In the writings of Søren Kierkegaard, Eric Voegelin, and René Girard, for example, we find the components of a theological anthropology that does actually comprehend human behaviors better than the secular alternatives that the Enlightenment has offered to us.

I know that some readers will question my use of the word "better" in the last sentence. They will say: "You are a religious person, so of course you will think that a religious interpretation of phenomena is better *from your point of view*. But that is simply a sign of your subjectivity. There is no neutral place from which we can say that one interpretation is better than another." I am aware of this criticism but I do not find it compelling. Imagine nineteenth-century abolitionists being told that their truth is only valid for them because it is *their point of view*. For the abolitionist to see that all human beings need to be treated with dignity because they are created in the image of God is not a private opinion, it is actually a key piece of theological science that is valid for all of humanity. That there can be a *theological science* is my presupposition in this book, and I believe that history will vindicate me on that point, just as it vindicated the abolitionists.

The idea that is missing from my interlocutor's critique is an awareness that there is a moral component to knowledge. Some forms of knowledge lead humanity down the path of moral development and others do not. The theological science that I am positing is not only more effective in interpreting the empirical data of human behavior, it is also more helpful in pointing toward the pathway of ethical development for the human race. Put differently, a form of understanding that is ethically constructive has that power because it interprets the phenomena more accurately.

Relativism maintains that the human condition has no definite structure. There are only varied opinions, but there is nothing substantive to be figured out. I maintain, on the contrary, that there is a structure of human existence that can actually be figured out. And when that comprehension is achieved it participates in the structure it has understood, which is human life as it has been created and is being created by God, the source of our being.

~

Part I of this book begins with an Introduction that outlines the three dimensions of existence: the vertical axis of God and nature, the horizontal plane of social existence, and the temporal trajectory of individual selfhood. This outline forms a foundation for understanding three key thinkers who have given us the basic tools we need to understand violence: Søren Kierkegaard, Eric Voegelin, and René Girard. This part is written primarily for students who are not already familiar with these authors; it introduces philosophical concepts that will be essential for understanding the second part of the book, which expresses the core of the argument.

In Part II I extensively develop the concept of the three dimensions of existence and use it as a lens through which our contemporary world can be interpreted. This section is headed by the Greek term *perichoresis* which means "mutual interrelations." This term is most commonly used in the context of the Christian doctrine of God's triune nature. The three persons, Father, Son, and Spirit, are described in Christian theology as present within each other's being and work. The Father begets the Son and breathes the Spirit. The Son communicates the Father's love in the power of the Spirit. The Spirit opens up human spirits to the Father by bearing witness to the work of the Son. In the context of this book, the term *perichoresis* indicates arguments that draw on Kierkegaard, Voegelin, and Girard, coordinating and weaving together their ideas in various ways. The Trinitarian resonance of the term is not mere window-dressing; it constitutes the heart of the argument, in that Voegelin helps us to understand our relation to the Father, Kierkegaard helps us to understand our relation to the Son, and Girard helps us to understand our relation to the Spirit.

I argue that the three dimensions of reality are a lens through which we *can* and in fact *must* interpret human behavior if we seek to comprehend violence. As a slight foretaste of my argument, I will mention here that the clashes between different personality patterns seen in the modern world are illuminated by awareness of the dimensions. "Fundamentalists" try to reside in the upper reaches of the vertical axis, living in God's back pocket; their rivalrous brothers the atheistic scientists dismiss transcendence and say that materiality is the only reality; egocentric individualists focus on the Self in defiance of the possibility of a more complex way of inhabiting the dimensions; revolutionaries such as Karl Marx tout the social, horizontal plane as the key to all of reality and as the solution to all human problems. In other words, I paint a picture of the dimensions as constituting limbs that people can climb out on when they seek to over-simplify the task of living in a complex world. But these limbs break off under the weight of unbalanced personalities. Our developmental task as human beings is to live in the Center, at the intersection of the dimensions, with an openness to the complexity that God calls us to participate in.

Another way of expressing this is to note that many authors work with some sort of dichotomy, such as: "*earlier* forms of thought are bad, *modern* forms of thought are good," or, "*the Bible* holds all truth, everything else is *vain philosophy*," or, "*we* are defenders of freedom, *they* are evildoers," or, as Nietzsche famously put it, "Christianity has replaced (and reversed) the dichotomy *the strong rule over the weak* with *the good rule over the evil*."[1] The dichotomy that I work with in this book is consciously intended to break down such dichotomies by suggesting that *simplistic* ways of thinking need to be replaced with *complex* ways of thinking. To refer to the somewhat long-in-the-tooth Wesleyan quadrilateral, for example, I would suggest that a person who has one primary source of knowledge, whether it is the Bible or tradition or reason or experience, is not as advanced intellectually as the person who seeks to hold these in creative tension: the Bible *and* tradition *and* reason *and* experience. These four terms are pointing to different aspects of the complexity of human life, and when this is not appreciated, the result is a stunted perception of reality.

As the text unfolds, I show how the concept of the three dimensions is refracted in many different ways in Christian thought: love of God, self, and neighbor; faith, hope, and love; Christ as king, prophet, and priest; Kierkegaard's "three spheres of existence"; Martin Luther King Jr.'s "three dimensions of a complete life," and so forth. In this sense, what I am arguing is not at all original. But the element of originality in my argument is seen in the tenacity with which I carry through this process of noticing and gathering refractions of the dimensions, and the way I apply this model of understanding to phenomena such as fundamentalism, modern individualism, and Marxism. I quote, for example, a psychologist who has analyzed the 9/11 hijackers as having a "vertically" oriented fundamentalist mindset. This fits my analysis perfectly and strengthens it, but the author I quote does not appear to have worked out the concept of the vertical, the individual, and the horizontal into a comprehensive anthropological vision. Many authors are seeing parts of the puzzle; my task is to put the pieces together so that an image begins to appear more clearly.

1. This is a paraphrase, rather than a quotation.

I can point to two items that are quite similar to my argument here: Mark Heim's *The Depth of the Riches: A Trinitarian Theology of Religious Ends*, and an essay by H. Richard Niebuhr. Heim argues that the major world religions, Buddhism, Islam, etc., are relating to various aspects of the triune God (without being consciously aware that this is what they are doing). His argument is very subtle and multi-faceted, and I cannot begin to summarize it here. His vision is similar to mine, but he is interpreting a different set of phenomena, and he is speaking in positive terms about human relations with the divine. My focus is negative; I am seeking to comprehend human psychopathologies as varying forms of rebellion against the persons of the Trinity.

H. Richard Niebuhr's essay "The Doctrine of the Trinity and the Unity of the Church" is another close parallel to my argument. Niebuhr argues that the history of Christian thought demonstrates that Christians often gravitate toward worship of the Father, or the Son, or the Holy Spirit, in such a manner that they end up with a "Unitarianism" of the Father, Son, or Spirit. One aspect of God is focused on and used as the primary orientation and the other aspects are downgraded or ignored. My argument proceeds along similar lines in that I am also noticing a contraction of thought when expansion and complexity are called for. A key difference between Niebuhr's argument and mine is that he is concerned primarily with Christian thought, whereas I venture farther afield in my comments on Islamist terrorists or Marxism or atheistic science, etc.

In addition to the topics already referred to, Part II also contains reflections on the relationship between theology, anthropology, and ethics; differing forms of time—cosmic, psychological, and cultural; the choices that we make without necessarily being aware that we are making them, which lead to different patterns of thought and action; theories of atonement; and the argument between the just war theory and pacifism. The reader who is thinking that these large topics cannot possibly be dealt with thoroughly in such a short book is exactly correct. My goal is not comprehensiveness and exhaustive analysis but intellectual stimulation. Nothing would make me happier than to have a reader take up a topic treated sketchily in this book and analyze it at greater depth.

Part III of the book consists of three essays that are rhetorical applications of insights from the second part. Chapter 6 focuses on interpreting the 9/11 attacks as a chief example of unbalanced fundamentalism in action. An essay by Kierkegaard, in which he critiques martyrdom, frames the discussion. Kierkegaard argues that we can distinguish between true and false forms of martyrdom by considering the deepest motivations of the martyr. Christ allowed himself to be killed to redeem others, to release them from the crushing weight of sin and accusation. He was a true martyr because he was not entangled in the mendacity of violent human culture. False martyrs die in order to accuse and condemn others and to "save" themselves by "obeying" an idolatrous god that they have themselves created.

Chapter 7 is a thought-experiment. What if President George W. Bush and his speech writers had been saturating themselves in the writings of those authors who have reflected most deeply on the roots of human violence (authors such as Kierkegaard, Voegelin, and Girard)? How would the speech he gave to Congress after the 9/11 attacks have been different if it were less of an example of unreflective nationalism and more of an example of seizing the moment to teach humanity about the psychology of violence?

Chapter 8 focuses on the anti-hypocrisy message of Christianity. Hypocrisy is accusing others of doing wrong when you yourself are doing wrong. It is thus the bedrock phenomenon that makes violence possible. Its plainly observable presence throughout human history enables us to see that hypocrisy is the human condition. It is the air we breathe. But we don't usually see it; we are hypocritical unconsciously. It is always possible that we could become more conscious; if we did, the ethical texture of human relationships would be transformed. Reflection on the long history of human corruption is depressing, but there is always more that can be said; there is always hope, which is the fruit of divine grace.

Acknowledgments

THE FOLLOWING PERSONS PROVIDED HELPFUL FEEDBACK DURING THE writing of this book: Gregory Sherwood, Mark Toulouse, Russell Reno, James Alison, David Gouwens, Jennifer Rike, Wayne Northey, and David Hart. This should not be interpreted to mean that these persons endorse each of the arguments contained herein, nor that they are responsible for the many deficiencies that remain. I also thank my students at Brite Divinity School and the parishioners of St. Gregory's Episcopal Church in Mansfield, Texas, who have been willing guinea pigs for the ideas in various contexts. My sincere thanks for all of the feedback and the goodwill.

Abbreviations for Books by Kierkegaard, Voegelin, and Girard

Girard, René. [DDN] *Deceit, Desire, and the Novel: Self and Other in Literary Structure.* Translated by. Yvonne Freccero. Baltimore: The Johns Hopkins University Press, 1965.

———. [TGR] *The Girard Reader*. Edited by James G. Williams. New York: Crossroad, 1996.

———. [ISS] *I See Satan Fall Like Lightning.* Translated by James G. Williams. Maryknoll, NY: Orbis, 2001.

———. [RFTU] *Resurrection from the Underground: Feodor Dostoevsky.* Translated by James G. Williams. New York: Crossroad, 1997.

———. [TS] *The Scapegoat.* Translated by Yvonne Freccero. Baltimore: The Johns Hopkins University Press, 1986.

———. [TH] *Things Hidden Since the Foundation of the World.* Translated by Stephen Bann and Michael Metteer. Stanford: Stanford University Press, 1987.

Kierkegaard, Søren. [CA] *The Concept of Anxiety: A Simple Psychologically Orienting Deliberation on the Dogmatic Issue of Hereditary Sin.* Translated by Reidar Thomte in collaboration with Albert B. Anderson. Princeton: Princeton University Press, 1980.

———. [CD] *Christian Discourses; The Crisis and A Crisis in the Life of an Actress.* Translated by Howard V. Hong and Edna H. Hong. Princeton: Princeton University Press, 1997.

———. [JP] *Søren Kierkegaard's Journals and Papers*, I–VII. Translated by Howard V. Hong and Edna H. Hong, assisted by Gregor Malantschuk. Bloomington: Indiana University Press, 1967–1978.

———. [PV] *The Point of View.* Translated by Howard V. Hong and Edna H. Hong. Princeton: Princeton University Press, 1998.

———. [PC] *Practice in Christianity.* Translated by Howard V. Hong and Edna H. Hong. Princeton: Princeton University Press, 1991.

———. [SUD] *The Sickness Unto Death: A Christian Psychological Exposition for Upbuilding and Awakening.* Translated by Howard V. Hong and Edna H. Hong. Princeton: Princeton University Press, 1983.

———. [TA] *Two Ages: A Literary Review.* Translated by Howard V. Hong and Edna H. Hong. Princeton: Princeton University Press, 1978.

———. [UDVS] *Upbuilding Discourses in Various Spirits.* Translated by Howard V. Hong and Edna H. Hong. Princeton: Princeton University Press, 1993.

———. [WA] *Without Authority.* Translated by Howard V. Hong and Edna H. Hong. Princeton: Princeton University Press, 1997.

———. [WL] *Works of Love*. Translated by Howard V. Hong and Edna H. Hong. Princeton: Princeton University Press, 1995.

Voegelin, Eric. [CWEV 5] *Modernity Without Restraint: The Political Religions, The New Science of Politics and Science, Politics, and Gnosticism*. Edited by Manfred Henningsen. The Collected Works of Eric Voegelin 5. Columbia: University of Missouri Press, 2000.

———. [CWEV 10] *Published Essays 1940–1952*. Edited by Ellis Sandoz. The Collected Works of Eric Voegelin 10. Baton Rouge: Louisiana State University Press, 2000.

———. [CWEV 12] *Published Essays 1966–1985*. Edited by Ellis Sandoz. The Collected Works of Eric Voegelin 12. Baton Rouge: Louisiana State University Press, 1990.

———. [CWEV 14] *Order and History, Volume I: Israel and Revelation*. Edited by Maurice P. Hogan. The Collected Works of Eric Voegelin 14. Columbia: University of Missouri Press, 2001.

———. [CWEV 17] *Order and History, Volume IV: The Ecumenic Age*. Edited by Michael Franz. The Collected Works of Eric Voegelin 17. Columbia: University of Missouri Press, 2001.

———. [CWEV 22] *History of Political Ideas, Volume IV*. Edited by David L. Morse and William M. Thompson. The Collected Works of Eric Voegelin 22. Columbia: University of Missouri Press, 1998.

———. [CWEV 31] *Hitler and the Germans*. Edited by Detlev Clemens and Brendan Purcell. The Collected Works of Eric Voegelin 31. Columbia: University of Missouri Press, 1999.

———. [CWEV 34] *Autobiographical Reflections*. Edited by Ellis Sandoz. The Collected Works of Eric Voegelin 34. Columbia: University of Missouri Press, 2006.

PART ONE

Scientists *of the* Spirit

The similarity between his life and mine occurred to me today. Just as he lives over there in Brazil, lost to the world, absorbed in excavating antediluvian fossils, so I live as if outside the world, absorbed in excavating Christian concepts—alas, and yet I am living in Christendom, where Christianity flourishes, stands in luxuriant growth with 1,000 clergymen, and where we are all Christians.

—Søren Kierkegaard [commenting on his cousin, the naturalist Wilhelm Lund], JP, 6:6652

Through my writings I hope to achieve the following: to leave behind me so accurate a characterization of Christianity and its relationships in the world that an enthusiastic, noble-minded young person will be able to find in it a map of relationships as accurate as any topographical map from the most famous institutes. I have not had the help of such an author. The old Church Fathers lacked one aspect, they did not know the world.

—Søren Kierkegaard, JP, 6:6283

If we are truly to learn to love our neighbors, we might start by simply trying to understand them.

—Imam Feisal Abdul Rauf, *What's Right with Islam*, 266

The invention of science is not the reason that there are no longer witch-hunts, but the fact that there are no longer witch-hunts is the reason that science has been invented. The scientific spirit, like the spirit of enterprise in an economy, is a by-product of the profound action of the Gospel text.

—René Girard, *The Scapegoat*, 204–5

Humanity cannot be explained in terms of itself.

—Olivier Clément, *On Human Being*, 10

For in a sense, the divine element in us moves everything. The starting point of reasoning is not reasoning, but something greater. What, then, could be greater even than knowledge and intellect but god?

—Aristotle, *Eudemian Ethics*, 1248a26–29

Q. Haven't you written a little something about language theory?
A. Yes.

Q. Could you summarize your thoughts on the subject?
A. No

Q. Why not?
A. It is not worth the trouble. What is involved in a theory of language is a theory of man, and people are not interested. Despite the catastrophes of this century and man's total failure to understand himself and deal with himself, people still labor under the illusion that a theory of man exists. It doesn't. As bad and confused as things are, they have to get even worse before people realize they don't have the faintest idea what sort of creature man is. Then they might want to know. Until then, one is wasting one's time.

—Walker Percy, *Signposts in a Strange Land*, 420.

1

Introduction

There are three dimensions of reality as it is experienced by human beings: the vertical axis, the horizontal plane, and the temporal trajectory. Along the vertical axis *God* is above and *nature* is below; the *neighbor* is found on the horizontal plane; and we exist as *individual selves* within the temporal trajectory.

The vertical axis has traditionally been called the hierarchy of being, the great chain of being, or in Latin the *scala naturae*. Matter and energy are at the bottom. Above that fundamental level we find the plants, then the non-sentient animals, the sentient animals, human beings, with God at the top. The natural sciences study what lies beneath human beings on this vertical axis. The upper part of the axis is the realm of theology, though theology is also concerned with nature as God's creation. Books on "the relationship between religion and science" are elucidating the questions that arise out of this vertical dimension of being. Key thinkers whose thought inhabits the vertical axis include Thomas Aquinas, whose masterful interpretation of the hierarchy of being and the ends of the human soul is the high point of medieval thought; Karl Barth, whose reassertion of the verticality of God's revelation was framed as a critique of modern thought's tendency to ignore or domesticate the transcendent dimension (in favor of the other two dimensions—selfhood and society); and Eric Voegelin, whose philosophy orients the human soul toward the divine source of life through an acceptance of its place *in between* God and nature, the transcendent and the immanent.[1]

1. On Thomas, see Pinckaers, *Sources of Christian Ethics*, chap. 17. See Barth's *Epistle to the Romans*. A sampling of Voegelin's thought can be found in *Published Essays, 1966–1985* (CWEV, 12). Voegelin discusses the hierarchy of being in CWEV, 12:289–91. He describes the hierarchy from the bottom up using these terms: Apeiron—Depth,

The horizontal dimension of reality points to our inescapable sociality as human beings. "One is a self only among other selves," as Charles Taylor argues.[2] When we consider the relationship between "church and state" or when we talk about culture, the family, or social ethics, we are aware of this dimension. In the modern university, the horizontal plane is studied by disciplines such as sociology, anthropology, law, political science, and economics. Karl Marx is a notable nineteenth-century proponent of this aspect of reality. In hindsight, we can see serious moral and philosophical flaws in his interpretation of human life; this has left the field open for much more perceptive treatments of the horizontal dimension, such as we have received from René Girard.

When I speak of the temporal dimension, I am pointing toward selfhood. There is a book by Phillip Cary, for example, that is called *Augustine's Invention of the Inner Self*. This title points effectively to the essence of this dimension. Charles Taylor's major work *The Sources of the Self* addresses this aspect of reality as a key historical development within what we call modernity. This temporal dimension stresses the idea that we live as individual selves in time, enacting our identities in the present moment between our personal and social past and the future we are moving into. Friedrich Nietzsche and Sigmund Freud are key modern commentators on this dimension, which is often the focus of study in psychology, philosophy, and literature departments. Within the realm of Christian thought, Kierkegaard's reflections on what he called "the category of the single individual" and "inwardness" are among the most profound illuminations of this dimension.

These are the three primary dimensions of reality as it is experienced by human beings. Visually presented:

Inorganic nature, Vegetative nature, Animal nature, Psyche—Passions, Psyche—Noetic, Divine Nous. In my view, Voegelin is the most substantive philosopher in the twentieth century; he is largely an undiscovered continent for the theological academy.

2. Taylor, *Sources of the Self*, 35. See also Cady, *Religion, Theology, and American Public Life*, 76: "The individual self needs others for the most basic task of becoming a self. Thus the dependence of the self upon society is inadequately reflected in social contract theories that presume the existence of selves prior to their real or imagined choice to enter into social relations."

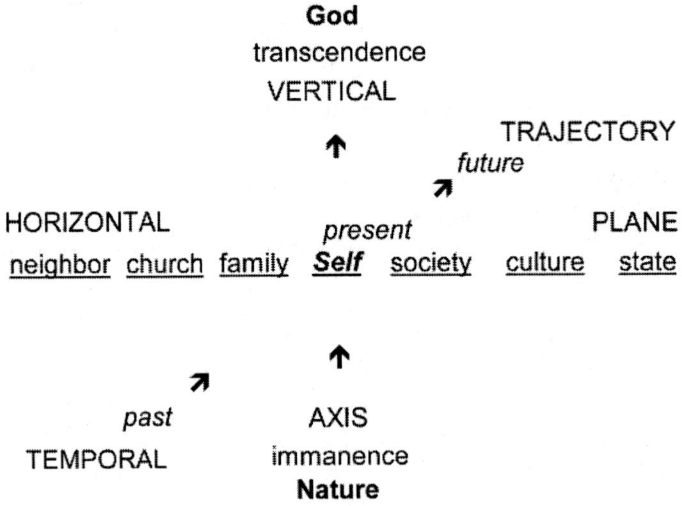

These three dimensions of reality are the milieu, the framework, in which we live as human beings. We do not make a choice about that; we live in these dimensions whether we want to or not. The question is not *if* we will inhabit the dimensions, but *how*.

Placing "God" at the top of the vertical axis can lead to a misunderstanding that I need to head off. It is not the case that "God" is located in one "place." God is the transcendent Creator who is everywhere within creation without being identified with it. This means that God also inhabits the temporal trajectory and the horizontal plane, without being limited in any way by them. I will amplify this line of thought later in the book.

~

Another perspective on the dimensions comes into view with these three statements: (1) there are some ways I am like everyone else, (2) there are some ways I am unique, and (3) there are some ways I am like some people and unlike other people.[3] (1) I am like all other human beings in terms of our basic physicality; we all need to breathe oxygen to survive; we have bones, muscles, skin, a brain, etc., that are expressions of our human DNA. This aspect constitutes the lower part of the vertical axis. The upper part of the vertical axis is expressed in theological language:

3. I was helped in formulating this perspective by a conversation with Woody Belangia.

we are all spiritual beings created in the image of God (Gen 1:26). (2) I am unique as an individual; I have my own memories, thoughts, emotions, plans, etc. Even if I had an identical twin, I would still be unique in this sense. (3) On the horizontal, social plane, I am like some people and unlike others when I consider factors such as gender, ethnicity, nationality, religion, etc. But all human beings are my neighbor. This quotation from Kierkegaard shows his awareness of these issues:

> From the beginning of the world, no human being exists or has existed who is the neighbor in the sense that the king is the king, the scholar the scholar, your relative your relative—that is, in the sense of exceptionality or, what amounts to the same thing, in the sense of dissimilarity—no, every human being is the neighbor. In being king, beggar, rich man, poor man, male, female, etc., we are not like each other—therein we are indeed different. But in being the neighbor we are all unconditionally like each other. Dissimilarity is temporality's method of confusing that marks every human being differently, but the neighbor is eternity's mark—on every human being. Take many sheets of paper, write something different on each one; then no one will be like another. But then again take each single sheet; do not let yourself be confused by the diverse inscriptions, hold it up to the light, and you will see a common watermark on all of them. In the same way the neighbor is the common watermark, but you see it only by means of eternity's light when it shines through the dissimilarity. (WL, 89)

When Kierkegaard speaks of eternity's light revealing the *neighbor*, he is describing the reality that we are all created in the image of God. The Atlantic slave trade was premised on the false idea that Africans were inferior to white Europeans. Africans were seen in the slave-holding ideology as being beasts of burden, like cattle or horses; they were not fully human. In the terms of our discussion thus far, the essential conceptual move was to place Africans lower than whites on the vertical axis, when in reality Africans should have been seen as fellow human beings (*neighbors*) on the horizontal plane, who are created in the image of God. Another chart:

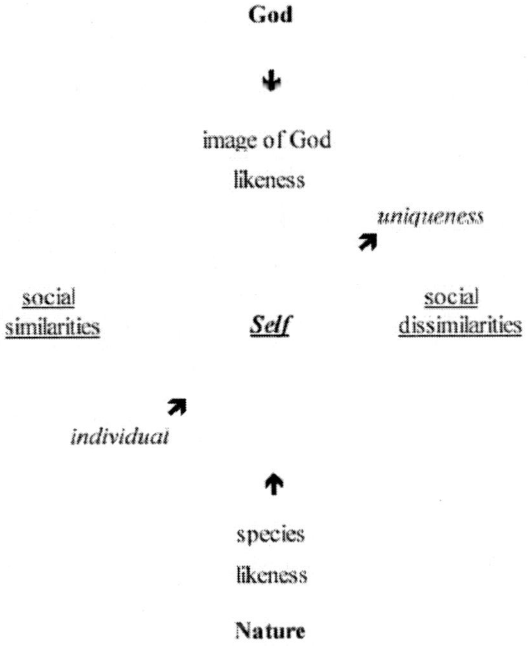

There are also the terms body, soul, and spirit, which have played key roles in traditional anthropological thinking. The body is obviously represented on the chart as the lower part of the vertical axis. Spirit can be associated with our relationship to God. Soul is our psychological constitution as individuals: our emotions, personality, will, and so forth.[4] René Girard has argued powerfully that we are intrinsically social beings. He calls this our "interdividuality."[5] This aspect of our human condition needs to be added to the discussion of body, soul, and spirit, which is often overly individualistic.

4. My reflections here are similar to, but not identical with, David Gushee's in *Only Human*, 51–56.

5. See *Things Hidden since the Foundation of the World.*

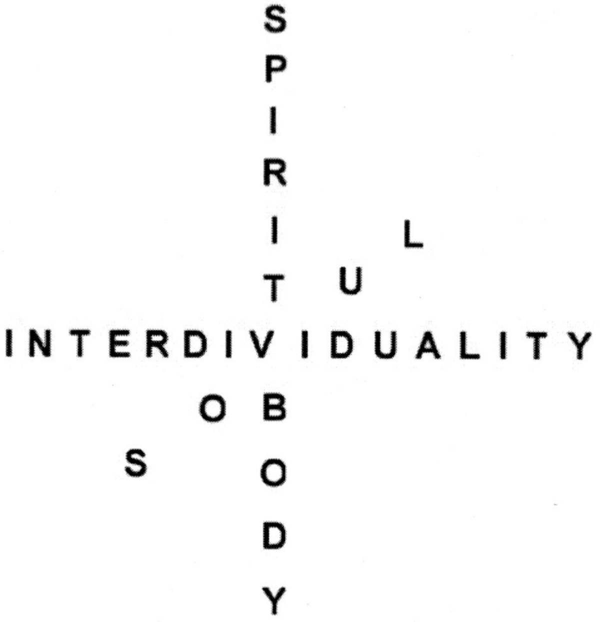

These various charts that I am presenting are different ways of describing the same basic structure of reality as it is experienced by human beings.

~

The dimensions of reality have been noticed and brought into articulation by various thinkers and in various scriptural texts. For example, when Jesus was asked which is the greatest commandment in the Law, he replied: "This is the first: Listen, Israel, the Lord our God is the one, only Lord, and you must love the Lord your God with all your heart, with all your soul, with all your mind and with all your strength. The second is this: You must love your neighbor as yourself. There is no commandment greater than these" (Mark 12:28–30). Jesus was laying out for us the three dimensions of reality: God, others, and the self. These are the three loves that constitute the core of healthy and balanced human existence. We will see in the following paragraphs some of many different ways that these basic dimensions have been expressed in the thinking of various authors.

The famous passage from the gospels just quoted was the chief inspiration for Martin Luther King Jr.'s speech on the theme "The Three Dimensions of a Complete Life."[6] He spoke of the three dimensions of life as its length, breadth, and height. The length of life refers to the individual's concern for his or her own welfare, achievements, plans, etc. Of course, there can be a negative form of this dimension when a person is overly egoistic and selfish, always using and abusing others for personal advantage. But there is also a positive form of this dimension when a person has a healthy self-love and self-understanding. By the breadth of life, King meant ethical relations with other human beings. He offered reflections on the parable of the Good Samaritan as a key biblical text that explores this dimension of life. He also spoke of the height of life as the relationship between human beings and God. This is the vertical dimension that needs to be shaped by faith and openness on the human side in order for the full flourishing of human life to occur. In other words, when this dimension is characterized by a positive relationship between the person and God, then the length and breadth of life also become positive and life-giving; loving God with all one's heart and soul leads to love of self and of neighbor. Negatively put, when one or more of these dimensions is stunted or warped in a person's life, there is diminishment of the soul.

In all encyclopedia articles that are written about Søren Kierkegaard, it is a requirement to mention his notion of the "spheres" or "stages" of existence. One of his books was entitled, in Danish, *Stadier paa Livets Vei*, which translates into English as *Stages on Life's Way*. The three *stadier* are the aesthetic, the ethical, and the religious. To translate *stadier* as "stages" has the unfortunate result, however, of implying that he is putting forward an interpretation of developmental psychology. First, a person is childish and aesthetic, living for self; second, a person matures and begins to take others into consideration and lives by a moral code; third, a person becomes religious as he or she approaches death and asks ultimate questions about the destiny of the human soul. But this notion of a natural process of human development is not what Kierkegaard intended at all. It is more helpful to use the word "spheres"

6. He presented versions of this talk at different times in different places. See "The Three Dimensions of a Complete Life" in *A Knock at Midnight*. King's sermon was based on a sermon preached by Phillips Brooks in the nineteenth century. See the sermon entitled "The Symmetry of Life" in *Phillips Brooks: Selected Sermons*.

of existence, or, as I am outlining the situation, "dimensions" of reality. These dimensions, the vertical (religious), the temporal trajectory of selfhood (aesthetic), and the horizontal (ethical) are with us always. As children or young adults or older adults we have the possibility of inhabiting these dimensions in many different ways, through a combination of environmental pressures, personal choices, and spiritual attractions. Much of Kierkegaard's authorship is devoted to exploring this complexity of human experience.

An earlier work by Kierkegaard, *Either/Or*, had also elucidated these three spheres of existence by allowing them to be spoken by imaginary characters: the young aesthete, Judge William, and the country priest. Kierkegaard was recasting in his own terms one of the most familiar stories of the New Testament: the Parable of the Prodigal Son.[7] The younger son in the story represents the dire consequences of living for self to the exclusion of all other values and obligations. His older brother adhered to the moral codes and customary patterns of loyalty to parents that form the backbone of ethical and social existence. The father in the story points toward a transcendent grace and forgiveness that covers all sins, both the sins of selfishness and those of self-righteousness. These three characters display the dimensions of reality: the temporal trajectory (selfhood), the horizontal plane (society), and the vertical axis (God).

Eric Voegelin provides a religiously oriented philosopher's perspective on the dimensions. At the beginning of *Order and History*, he lays out the structure of his interpretation of human existence:

> God and man, world and society form a primordial community of being. The community with its quaternarian structure is, and is not, a datum of human experience. It is a datum of experience in so far as it is known to man by virtue of his participation in the mystery of its being. It is not a datum of experience in so far as it is not given in the manner of an object of the external world but is knowable only from the perspective of participation in it. (CWEV 14:39)

What Voegelin calls "quaternarian" correlates with the dimensions as I have articulated them. God and world constitute what I have labeled

7. See Bellinger, "Kierkegaard's *Either/Or*."

the vertical dimension. "Man" refers to selfhood, and society is the horizontal.

The history of political thought in the Western world can be viewed according to a three-fold pattern. *Monarchy* is the ancient principle for organizing society. Power flows from the top down. The ruler rules and the subjects are subject. But in the wake of the American and French revolutions, monarchy was dethroned in favor of *democracy*. Government ought to be of the people, by the people, and for the people. Power flows from the bottom up through the ballot box. But what if the majority is oppressive toward a minority group or toward individuals who think differently from the herd? The notion that "the crowd" can be wrong places democracy in a dubious light. The "rights" of individuals need to be protected from the power of the state, regardless of whether the state consists of elected officials or not. Thus a third political principle is placed in tension with the other two: *individual autonomy*. We can see once again in these possibilities the vertical, the horizontal, and the selfhood dimensions of reality. The clash of these dimensions, when they are inhabited in an unbalanced way, produces many dramatic conflicts in human history.

Another refraction of the dimensions is seen in what is an admittedly oversimplified view of the main branches of Christianity. Roman Catholicism can be viewed as inhabiting the hierarchical, vertical pattern. It has often been pointed out that its structure mirrors the political structure of the Roman Empire, with the Pope replacing Caesar. The term *pontifex maximus* is in fact a title that was applied to emperors such as Augustus.[8] Protestantism tends to focus on the dimension of individual selfhood. This can be seen in both its conservative forms, which emphasize the salvation of individual souls, and in its liberal forms, which tend to affirm modern notions of individual autonomy. Eastern Orthodoxy adopts a more collegial, horizontal view of the office of bishop, and it seeks to foster a strong sense of ecclesial spirituality. The Russian term *sobornost* could be translated as "togetherness" or "communality"; this term is often used to point to the essence of Orthodoxy as providing an alternative to Western individualism.

8. This should not be construed as a criticism. The *lack* of a central executive authority in the church can lead to fragmentation, as contemporary Anglicanism demonstrates.

An awareness of the dimensions can be seen in Reinhold Niebuhr. Consider, for example, this passage from *The Nature and Destiny of Man*:

> The Bible defines sin in both religious and moral terms. The religious dimension of sin is man's rebellion against God, his effort to usurp the place of God. The moral and social dimension of sin is injustice. The ego which falsely makes itself the center of existence in its pride and will-to-power inevitably subordinates other life to its will and thus does injustice to other life.[9]

The vertical and horizontal dimensions are clearly indicated, with "the ego" pointing to the dimension of individual selfhood.

In his book *The Responsible Self*, Reinhold's brother H. Richard Niebuhr outlines three approaches to thinking about Christian ethics.[10] The labels he uses are man-the-maker, man-the-citizen, and man-the-answerer. Man-the-maker indicates our ability as human beings to conceive of goals and purposes and then to choose the means we will use to accomplish those goals. Human beings are inwardly impelled and guided in this perspective. Man-the-citizen lives under laws and commandments that are traditionally understood as coming down from above; the "above" may be understood as God or as the earthly ruler. Or, the laws can be understood as coming from "below" (natural law). From a theological point of view, the laws from "below" are actually also from "above" in the sense that they derive ultimately from the Creator. Man-the-answerer is Niebuhr's articulation of an alternative approach to ethical thinking that focuses on human relationships. "The idea or pattern of responsibility, then, may summarily and abstractly be defined as the idea of an agent's action as response to an action upon him in accordance with his interpretation of the latter action and with his expectation of response to his response; and all of this in a continuing community of agents."[11] This approach is horizontal in the sense that it points to society as the key context that shapes our thoughts and actions. Niebuhr also uses the terms "teleology" and "deontology" for the first two approaches, which allows us to visualize his analysis in this chart:

9. Niebuhr, *Nature and Destiny of Man*, I:179.

10. Niebuhr, *Responsible Self*, chap. 1.

11. Ibid., 65.

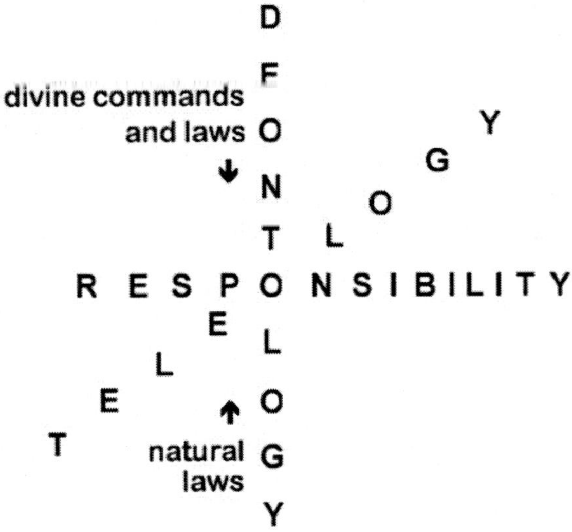

In many ways, my analyses and arguments in this book are "stalking" H. Richard Niebuhr in the sense that I am asking many of the same questions that he was asking in *Christ and Culture* and *The Responsible Self*. The reader who is familiar with those books will recognize the similarities, but also the substantive differences in the way I answer those questions.

In *Christ and Culture*, Niebuhr outlines five "types" within the history of Christian ethical thinking. These can be correlated with the basic chart (see page 3 above) of the dimensions of reality. "Christ against culture" and "Christ of culture" are the horizontal types; these match up with "church" and "state" in the chart. (The German Christians who supported Hitler would have been a perfect example of "Christ of culture" but for some odd reason Niebuhr chose not to mention them, even though he was writing in the wake of WW II.) "Christ above culture" is clearly the vertical, natural law, Thomistic dimension. "Christ and culture in paradox" points to the tension between the trajectory of selfhood and the horizontal plane. The individual is the recipient of grace, yet he or she must still live within the fallen social and political plane. And "Christ transforming culture" is reaching toward the idea that the dimensions are synthesized by the growing self who plays a transformative role in the cultural setting. Critics of Niebuhr have pointed out that there is a contradiction between his apparent neutrality in describing the types, and his clear preference for the fifth type.[12] The concept of the dimensions and their integration as I am articulating it in this book shows the validity of this criticism. Niebuhr's argument would have been strengthened if he had made a clearer normative case for the fifth type, which is transforming precisely because it holds the dimensions in creative tension in a world that prefers living out on the limbs of the dimensions rather than in *the center*.

This is the direction Niebuhr was heading in his intriguing essay "The Doctrine of the Trinity and the Unity of the Church." In the essay he argues that the history of Christianity shows evidence of "unitarianisms" of the Father, the Son, and the Spirit, in which one person of the Trinity is emphasized and the others are denied, downgraded, or ignored, leading to various distortions or heresies. His conclusion lobbies for a more complex vision, which expresses well what I am also trying to achieve in this book:

> The Trinitarianism of the whole church must undertake to state what is implicit in the faith and knowledge of all of its parts though it is not explicit in any one of them. It must undertake to correct the over-emphases and partialities of the members of the whole not by means of a new over-emphasis but by means of a synthesized formula in which all the partial insights and convictions are combined. A doctrine of the Trinity, so formulated, will never please any one part of the church but it will be an ecumenical doctrine providing not for the exclusion of heretics but for their inclusion in the body on which they are actually dependent. Truth, after all, is not the possession of any individual or of any party or school, but is represented, insofar as it can be humanly represented, only by the whole dynamic and complementary work of the company of knowers and believers.[13]

This is well put, and it outlines a task for theology that is just as relevant today as when Niebuhr first penned these lines in 1946.

Two other recently published books can be mentioned as examples of authors using the idea of the dimensions of reality as a central interpretive tool. *Dimensions of Evil* by Terry Cooper provides an overview

12. See Yoder's comments in *Authentic Transformation*, 40–43.

13. Niebuhr, "Doctrine of the Trinity and the Unity of the Church," 383–84.

of modern perspectives on natural and moral evil. The book is structured around three main loci: discussions of natural evil in the wake of Darwin's thought, psychological interpretations of crimes committed by individuals, and psychological interpretations of social (systemic) evil as seen in examples such as Naziism. Also of note is a big book (623 pages) by Eric Johnson, entitled *Foundations for Soul Care: A Christian Psychology Proposal.* Johnson articulates a "complex model of human life" that considers the interrelationships between four "orders of meaning" which correspond to what I call dimensions. His orders are the biological, the psychosocial, the ethical, and the spiritual. When one reads his description of the orders, it becomes clear that the biological and the spiritual are pointing to the vertical axis of God and nature; the psychosocial is pointing to what I have labeled as the horizontal plane; and the ethical points to what I call the trajectory of the individual through time. He describes the ethical by referring to concepts such as personal agency, free will, creativity, and capacity for virtue, vice, and character. Johnson's argument parallel's mine in two other key respects: it is also an explicitly Trinitarian psychology, and it draws heavily on Kierkegaard.

~

The survey of the dimensions that I have just completed has laid the groundwork for the second part of this book, where I will argue that the dimensions are lenses that enable us to see the roots of violence more clearly. But before we get there, I will spend more time introducing the thought of Kierkegaard, Voegelin, and Girard. These three thinkers have distinct emphases on the selfhood, vertical, and horizontal dimensions. Looking at them more carefully will add depth and weight to what I have just been outlining in a sketchy way.

2

Askesis: Introduction to Søren Kierkegaard

Life and Writings

SØREN KIERKEGAARD WAS BORN IN 1813, IN COPENHAGEN, DENMARK, as the seventh child of a wealthy businessman. His father was a self-educated man who had a brooding, deeply religious spirit. The father's pietism and philosophical interests had a great impact on his youngest son, Søren, who went on to become one of the most important figures in modern Christian thought.

Søren Kierkegaard was a bright student, and he received a high-quality private school education. By the time he was seventeen, he could read Hebrew, Greek, Latin, German, and French, as well as his native Danish. He entered the University, where his father hoped that he would study to become a pastor. But Kierkegaard was more interested in studying literature and philosophy, and he adopted the carefree, expensive lifestyle of a prodigal son. He wrestled deeply with religious ideas, however, and at the age of twenty-five he had a profound conversion experience. He was reconciled with his father shortly before the latter's death, and he dedicated himself to the cause of Christian faith for the rest of his life.

The Kierkegaard family was deeply touched by tragedy. By the time Søren was twenty-five, five of his six siblings had died, as well as his mother and father. Søren himself did not expect to live past the age of thirty. (As it was, he died at the age of forty-two in 1855.) He went on to complete the prerequisites for ordination in the Lutheran church, but he never did become ordained. Through his writings, he became a kind of pastor-at-large to the country of Denmark. In 1841 he earned an advanced degree in philosophy, with a dissertation on *The Concept of Irony: With Constant Reference to Socrates.*

At the age of twenty-seven he became engaged to Regine Olsen. For the next year he agonized within himself as to whether or not he had made a mistake. He broke off the engagement, believing that a marriage between them would not be viable, due to his personal eccentricities and his intense preoccupation with becoming an author. This engagement and its dissolution became one of the main inspirations for his subsequent authorship.

Since he had inherited a large sum of money from his father's estate, he was able to embark on a career as an independent author. Between the years of 1843 and 1851 he published a stream of books that are remarkable in their number, literary complexity, philosophical perception, and theological profundity. Since he wrote in Danish, he was only noticed at first by a handful of Danish intellectuals. It was not until the twentieth century that he became a well-known and widely read figure on the Western intellectual scene, in the wake of his writings being translated into German, French, and English.

His authorship can be divided into two time periods and six writing styles. The first time period is referred to as his "first authorship," from 1843 to 1846; the second period consists of works written between 1847 and 1855, which are known as his "second authorship." The first authorship consists primarily of pseudonymous works that were published under pen names such as Victor Eremita, Judge William, Hilarius Bookbinder, and Johannes Climacus. These pen names were attached to imaginary authors whose viewpoints did not necessarily coincide with Kierkegaard's own viewpoint. A novelist writes a novel by imagining characters and placing them in a setting and a plot. Kierkegaard imagined characters and had these characters write books. An understanding of this point is crucial for the project of interpreting his writings. In his own voice, Kierkegaard said, "If it should occur to anyone to want to quote a particular passage from the books, it is my wish, my prayer, that he will do me the kindness of citing the respective pseudonymous author's name, not mine" (CUP, 627). After publishing his work *Concluding Unscientific Postscript*, Kierkegaard intended to end his career as an author. But at that time a satirical newspaper called *The Corsair* began to lampoon him, at Kierkegaard's own request. As a result, Kierkegaard became a laughingstock in Danish society, and this incident spurred him on to continue writing. The books he wrote subsequently have become known as his second authorship; they are mainly religious works, published under his own name.

Kierkegaard's authorship can also be divided into six main writing styles. The six categories are as follows, with a listing of the titles that fit into them:

1. Criticism: *Early Polemical Writings* [c. 1838], *The Concept of Irony* [1841], *Two Ages* [1846], *The Book on Adler* [c. 1847], *The Crisis and a Crisis in the Life of an Actress* [1848].
2. Fiction: *Either/Or* [1843], *Repetition* [1843], *Fear and Trembling* [1843], *Prefaces* [1844], *Stages on Life's Way* [1845].
3. Philosophy of Religion: *The Concept of Anxiety* [1844], *Philosophical Fragments* [1844], *Concluding Unscientific Postscript* [1846].
4. Pastoral Theology: *Eighteen Upbuilding Discourses* [1843–1844], *Three Discourses on Imagined Occasions* [1845], *Upbuilding Discourses in Various Spirits* [1847], *Works of Love* [1847], *Christian Discourses* [1848], miscellaneous later discourses [1849–1855].
5. Polemical Theology: *The Sickness Unto Death* [1849], *Practice in Christianity* [1850], *For Self-Examination* [1851], *Judge for Yourself!* [c. 1851–1852], *The Moment* and miscellaneous later writings [1855].
6. Autobiographical Works: *The Point of View for My Work as an Author* [c. 1848], Journals and Papers [1829–1855].

The first category contains works of literary, philosophical, cultural, and religious criticism. The second category contains works that are "novelistic" in character; they focus on the boundaries between different spheres of existence, such as the aesthetic and the ethical, and the ethical and the religious; they often focus on the subject of marriage; they can be traced back to Kierkegaard's relationship with Regine. The third category consists of pseudonymous works of a highly philosophical character; they address the themes of original sin, the Incarnation, and Christian existence. The fourth category includes Kierkegaard's religious/upbuilding discourses; these are in effect sermons, but they are meant to be read in published form rather than preached in church;

they are addressed to a general audience and they speak in a pastoral and comforting, yet challenging, tone. The fifth category contains late works in which Kierkegaard analyzes and speaks out prophetically against what he sees as the spiritual bankruptcy of Western Christendom. The sixth category is made up of his remarkable autobiographical work, *The Point of View for My Work as an Author*, and of his voluminous journals, in which he carries on a running commentary on his life and times and the inner workings of his writing career.

These various writing styles can be understood as growing out of Kierkegaard's relationships with the various kinds of people he knew. His "fiction" was addressed to the literary intellectuals of his day, but it also grew out of his engagement to Regine; his "philosophy of religion" was directed at the philosophers and theologians of his time, who were largely under the sway of Hegelianism; his pastoral theology was intended for a general audience; his polemical theology was directed to the leaders of the state church, Bishops Mynster and Martensen. There is also a sense in which everything he wrote was addressed to God. Thus his authorship reveals the intricate nexus of relationships in which he lived. (This nexus of relationships is well-illustrated in the volume *Encounters with Kierkegaard*, edited by Bruce Kirmmse, which contains all of the extant accounts of Kierkegaard by those who knew him.)

During the last months of his life, Kierkegaard carried out a relentless verbal attack on the state church in Denmark, which he judged as having departed from the path of genuine New Testament Christianity. He finally collapsed one day in the street, was carried to a hospital, and died about a month later. His older brother Peter, the only other surviving member of the family, went on later to become a bishop in that same state church.

Kierkegaard Graffiti

Kierkegaard was *widely read* in the twentieth century, but it is far from clear that he was *widely understood*. In most cases, his interpreters and critics laid over his writings a heavy layer of their own biases, preoccupations, and jargon. When authors attempted to criticize him, their criticisms were often completely contradictory to each other. One person, for example, would say that Kierkegaard was too aesthetic; another would say that he was anti-aesthetic. One person would say that he was too individualistic; another would say that he was authoritarian and fascistic; yet another would say that he was the most anti-fascist thinker in the modern world (a view I endorse). One person would say that he was anti-feminist; another would say that his thought is a great gift to feminism. Most contributions to this jungle of criticism are examples of the phenomenon I refer to as Kierkegaard Graffiti. Just as the vandal who spraypaints a building hastily in the dark and then runs away has no real appreciation for the architecture of the building he is defacing, so also did Kierkegaard's deep and complex authorship become the victim of misconstrual and slander by people who did not expend the time and effort required for developing a clear understanding of his central concerns. Just one example of this graffiti is the phrase "the leap of faith" which is considered by many authors of encyclopedia articles to be the perfect summary of "Kierkegaard's philosophy." It turns out that he never used that phrase anywhere in his writings.[1] The fact that Kierkegaard graffiti can be produced by scholars who have studied his writings extensively and perhaps even written dissertations on him is a sign that his authorship is a very difficult exegetical challenge, but that does not relieve the producers of the graffiti of their responsibility to speak accurately.[2]

Central Themes in Kierkegaard's Thought

In my view, an accurate summary of Kierkegaard would proceed along these lines. Kierkegaard understood the world as the sphere of the creative activity of God. He took very seriously the fundamental biblical theme that God creates the universe through speech. Everything that exists does so because God is speaking it into existence. The human soul is that unique place in all of nature where the voice of God can be heard and responded to consciously. The animals, vegetables, and minerals are simply given from God's hand without self-consciousness; but human beings are able to be aware of their divine source. We are not only spoken into existence, but we also have the ability to be hearers of

1. See McKinnon, "Kierkegaard and the 'Leap of Faith.'"

2. This is a very short list of some of the graffiti erasers, the competent works on Kierkegaard: Gouwens, *Kierkegaard as Religious Thinker*; Malantschuk, *Kierkegaard's Thought*; Eller, *Kierkegaard and Radical Discipleship*; Evans, *Søren Kierkegaard's Christian Psychology*; Ferreira, *Love's Grateful Striving*; Kirmmse, *Kierkegaard in Golden Age Denmark*; Westphal, *Kierkegaard's Critique of Reason and Society.*

that speech. This is our transcendent nobility as human beings, but it is also our peril.

Just as we are superior to the lower animals because we can respond to our Creator consciously, so also can we sink below them into the abyss of sin. The psychology of the animals is set, determined. But our psychology is rooted in freedom. Another way of putting this is to say that we do not simply exist; we are coming into existence. Our character is not set in stone; our character is shaped by our experiences, our fears and anxieties, our relationships with other people, and by our Creator, whose voice is calling us forward into greater maturity as human beings. There are various possibilities open to us if we choose to allow our self to develop in this direction or that direction. The most basic choice that presents itself to us at all times concerns our response to the divine call of creation. We can respond positively to this call and allow ourselves to be drawn forward into the fullness of selfhood that God intends for us, or we can attempt to deafen ourselves to God's voice and seize control of our selfhood. This is precisely what Adam and Eve did, and what we all do as their children. They sought to "become as God," to usurp the place of God as the shaper of their future. In the same way, human beings down through the centuries have tried to manage and contain their angst by turning away from God in an attempt to avoid the pain of personal growth. We find it easier to reinforce the status quo of our souls and our societies than to allow the continuing event of creation to make, unmake, and remake us.

When we start down this path of deafening ourselves to the voice of God, we quickly develop a psychological inertia. Our commitment to avoiding the pain of growth is so strong that we organize our character and our societies around that commitment. When we cut ourselves off from the fullness of what the future could hold for us, we inevitably become stunted and misshapen as persons. Instead of living creatively in the tensions of existence before God, such as freedom and necessity, or the eternal and the temporal, we careen in one direction or the other, seeking then to fortify ourselves within one of those poles of existence. What we are seeking to evade above all else is the possibility that we could actually become ourselves before God. Instead of moving in faith into the fullness of life that God calls us to, we choose to follow the pathway that Kierkegaard calls "the sickness unto death."

As I said above, Kierkegaard is sometimes accused of being "individualistic," and is written off as an unhelpful thinker on that basis. The ineptitude of this criticism is actually very instructive, because it allows for the shape of his thought to be seen more clearly. Consider a passage such as this:

> In our age the principle of association (which at best can have validity with respect to material interest) is not affirmative but negative; it is an evasion, a dissipation, an illusion, whose dialectic is as follows: as it strengthens individuals, it vitiates them; it strengthens by numbers, by sticking together, but from the ethical point of view this is weakening. Not until the single individual has established an ethical stance despite the whole world, not until then can there be any question of genuinely uniting; otherwise it gets to be a union of people who separately are weak, a union as unbeautiful and depraved as a child-marriage. (TA, 106)

Kierkegaard is praising the "single individual" and criticizing sociality; therefore the label "individualistic" must be appropriate, in the eyes of his critics. But they always ignore phrases such as "genuinely uniting" because these phrases ruin the simplistic reading. Kierkegaard does not see the single individual as an end but as a doorway that opens onto a new form of sociality. This can be illustrated with an hourglass turned on its side. On the left side there is the "crowd," which is human sociality in its corrupted form. The crowd is a product of rebellion against God and resistance to spiritual growth. To become a single individual is to leave this sphere and move into the sphere of positive sociality that is characterized by love of God, self, and neighbor. Visually presented:

Rebellion against God		Faith in God
Resistance to spiritual growth	Becoming a single individual → The narrow pass →	Hope, openness to God's future
The crowd is untruth, hatred and violence		Love of neighbor

Notice how the left side of this image is clearly laid out in quotations such as these:

> Just as nowadays attempts are made in so many ways to emancipate people from all bonds, also beneficial ones, so also attempts are made to emancipate the emotional relationships between people from the bond that binds one to God and binds one in everything, in every expression of life. In connection with love, there is the desire to teach people something totally new, something for which the now old-fashioned Holy Scripture already has the characteristic expression—there is the desire to teach people the freedom that is "without God in the world". . . .
>
> As a reward for such presumption, all existence will in that way probably come closer and closer to being transformed into doubt or into a vortex. What, after all, is the Law, what is the Law's requirement of a person? Well, that is for people to decide. Which people? Here doubt begins. . . . In order to have to begin to act, the individual must first find out from "the others" what the Law's requirement is, but each one of these others must in turn as an individual find this out from "the others." In this way all human life transforms itself into one big excuse—is this perhaps the great, matchless common enterprise, the great achievement of the human race? The category "the others" becomes fanciful, and the fancifully sought determination of what constitutes the Law's requirement is a false alarm. . . .
>
> But to what can we compare that confused state just described? Is it not a mutiny? Or should we hesitate to call it that if at a given time the whole human race was guilty of it and we then add, note well, that it is a mutiny against God? Or is morality subordinated to coincidence in this way: when a great number do what is wrong, or we all do it, then this wrong is the right? This explanation would in turn be nothing more that a repetition of the thinking of the mutiny or its thoughtlessness, because then it ultimately is people who determine the Law's requirement instead of God. Therefore the one who forgets this not only becomes personally guilty of rebellion against God but also contributes his share to the mutiny's gaining the upper hand. . . .
>
> Only when all of us, each one separately, receive our orders at one place, if I may put it this way, and then each one separately unconditionally obeys the same orders, only then are there substance and purpose and truth and actuality in existence. . . . When this is the case, there is durability in existence, because God has a firm hold on it. There is no vortex, because each

> individual begins, not with "the others" and therefore not with evasions and excuses, but begins with the God-relationship and therefore stands firm and thereby also stops, as far as he reaches, the dizziness that is the beginning of mutiny. (WL, 114–18)

The passage just quoted presents very clearly the image of the modern world as taking (vertical) rebellion against God as its starting point; the (horizontal) chaos that results is plain for all to see; the antidote is genuine relationship with God.

The next quotation establishes a clear connection between human resistance to the possibility of spiritual growth and violent actions:

> *How Did It Happen That Christ Was Put to Death?*
>
> I can answer this in such a way that with the same answer I show what Christianity is.
>
> What is "spirit"? (And Christ is indeed spirit, his religion is of the spirit.) Spirit is: to live as if dead (to die to the world). So far removed is this mode of existence from the natural man that it is quite literally worse for him than simply dying.
>
> The natural man can tolerate it for an hour when it is introduced very guardedly at the distance of the imagination—yes, then it even pleases him. But if it is moved any closer to him, so close that it is presented in dead earnestness as a demand upon him, then the self-preservation instinct of the natural life is aroused to such an extent that it becomes a regular fury, as happens through drinking. In this state of derangement he demands the death of the man of spirit or rushes upon him to slay him. (JP, 4:4360)

When God comes to us in the person of Christ, what do we do? We could allow him to heal us of our "sickness unto death" and lead us back into the process of creation. But we don't do that. We are enraged by the voice that judges our smallness and choice of mediocrity. We must silence this voice in order to protect ourselves from its disturbing call. We stop up our ears and rush upon Jesus to kill him. Kierkegaard is pointing us in the direction we must look if we seek to understand the violence that erupts from the depths of the human soul. Violence is not "senseless"; it has a purpose. It seeks to fend off the possibility that always lies before us—the possibility that we could become the mature, loving human beings that God wants us to be.

When human beings are in rebellion against God and in flight from their own true selfhood, they form what Kierkegaard calls at various times a false "alliance," a crowd, a mob, or a wolf pack. This phenomenon is very clearly described in his important but rarely read essay on the theme "the crowd is untruth."[3] I wish I could quote the entire essay, but I present only one snippet:

> A crowd—not this or that, one now living or long dead, a crowd of the lowly or of nobles, of rich or poor, etc., but in its very concept—is untruth, since a crowd either renders the single individual wholly unrepentant and irresponsible, or weakens his responsibility by making it a fraction of his decision . . . For every single individual who escapes into the crowd, and thus flees in cowardice from being a single individual, contributes his share of cowardice to "the cowardice," which is: the crowd. Take the highest, think of Christ—and the whole human race, all human beings, which were ever born and ever will be born; the situation is the single individual, as an individual, in solitary surroundings alone with him; as a single individual he walks up to him and spits on him: the human being has never been born and never will be, who would have the courage or the impudence for it; this is the truth. But since they remain in a crowd, they have the courage for it—what frightening untruth.

Kierkegaard's suspicion of social relations when they arise out of alienation from God is very clearly laid out here. The selections we have just covered have given us glimpses of how Kierkegaard views the vertical (mutiny against God), selfhood (resistance to the call to grow), and the horizontal (the crowd is untruth).

Notice how the following passages show the interconnectedness in Kierkegaard's thinking of love of God, self, and neighbor:

> It is still the greatest, the *roomiest* part of the world, although spatially the smallest, this kingdom of love in which we can all be landholders without the need of one person's holding crowding another's—yes, it rather extends another's holdings. . . . On the other hand, the kingdom of anger and hate—how small it is in its egotistic isolation and how great the space it demands—the whole world is not spacious enough, because it has no room *for others.* (JP, 1:875)

3. Published in *The Point of View*, 105–12. My translation is available on the Internet here: http://www.ccel.org/ccel/kierkegaard/untruth/files/untruth.html. The following quotation is from my translation.

> When one denies God, he does God no harm but destroys himself; when one mocks God, he mocks himself. (JP, 2:1349)

> God is not my Father or any man's Father in a special way (frightful presumptuousness and madness!); no, he is Father only in the sense of being the Father of all. When I hate someone or deny that God is his Father, it is not he who loses but I—then I have no Father. (JP, 2:1413)

> Love to God and love to neighbor are like two doors that open simultaneously, so that it is impossible to open the one without opening the other, and impossible to shut one without also shutting the other. (JP, 3:2434)

That we are called by God to become mature, loving human beings is the central theme of Kierkegaard's *Works of Love*. This work is an extended meditation on the creative speech of God, which comes to us very concretely in the words of Christ: "You shall love your neighbor as yourself." This commandment is both a critique of human culture as it is currently constituted and a call to live as agents of God's love, as illustrated in this passage:

> Everyone who in despair has clung to one or another of the dissimilarities of earthly life so that he centers his life in it, not in God, also demands that everyone who belongs to the same dissimilarity must hold together with him—not in the good (because the good forms no alliance, does not unite two nor hundreds nor all people in an alliance), but in an ungodly alliance against the universally human. The one in despair calls it treason to want to have fellowship with others, with all people. . . . Whoever then will love the neighbor, whoever thus does not concern himself with removing this or that dissimilarity, or with eliminating all of them in a worldly way, but devoutly concerns himself with permeating his dissimilarity with the sanctifying thought of Christian equality—that person easily becomes like one who does not fit into earthly life here, not even with so-called Christendom; he is easily exposed to attacks from all sides; he easily becomes like a lost sheep among ravenous wolves. Everywhere he looks, he naturally sees the dissimilarities . . . and those who in a worldly way have clung firmly to a temporal dissimilarity, whatever it may be, are like ravenous wolves. (WL, 73)

The social system we are born into will decree that we should "love," or have preference for, some people, and hate or ignore others. But when we hear the command and respond to it, we are lifted up by our Creator onto a higher plane on which we are able to love concretely, consistently, and unselfishly. Our response to the divine command gives us our true identity as creatures, which is something that cannot be manufactured by our culture.

To summarize, Kierkegaard paints a picture of the human situation that can be likened to an oscillating fan. The three positions of the oscillation are society, individual selfhood, and relation to God. In our fallen sinfulness, our individuality is underdeveloped and we live on the social level, mimicking others who belong to a "crowd." But we have the potential to be pried loose, to be disentangled from the crowd. If this happens, we will become individual selves existing before God. (This is Kierkegaard's main *emphasis* as a thinker, though he is obviously aware of all three dimensions.) The fan will shift from the horizontal plane, through emerging selfhood, to the vertical axis. But Kierkegaard is not a Gnostic seeking to flee from the world. Our relation to God sends us back into the world to love the neighbor. The fan oscillates down to the horizontal plane once more, but the individual has been transformed. Instead of being motivated by spiritual sloth, the individual is motivated by faith, hope, and love. The process of spiritual transformation that I am pointing to with the image of the fan can be summarized with the Greek word *askesis*, which originally meant athletic training or practice, as in "training for the Olympics." It was also used in a military context, as in "basic training." In the early centuries of Christianity, the word was transposed into a spiritual context, referring to the exercises of the monks and nuns as they sought separation from the world for the purpose of greater openness to God. The English word *asceticism* is derived from the Greek root in this spiritual usage. Kierkegaard's thought can be seen as an expression of this central Christian motif. One of his key works, for example, is called *Practice in Christianity*. The Danish word *Indøvelse*, translated as *practice*, or as *training* in the earlier edition, is the direct equivalent of *askesis*.

For Kierkegaard, spiritual growth is a Christological event. We become individuals before God by modeling ourselves after Christ, who is the prototype of true selfhood. When this point is not understood, critics interpret Kierkegaard's comments on "the single individual" out of context and accuse him of "individualism." In reality, Kierkegaard's understanding of what it means to be an individual *before God*, truly loving *the neighbor*, shows that the ultimate antidote for modern individualism is Christian *askesis*.

3

Anamnesis: Introduction to Eric Voegelin

Life

Eric Voegelin was born in Cologne, Germany, in 1901. He studied with the Faculty of Law at the University of Vienna, earning an advanced degree in political science in 1922. During the years 1924–1927 he pursued post-doctoral studies at Columbia University, Harvard, the University of Wisconsin, and in Paris at the Sorbonne. This study tour, especially the American portion of it, proved to be very important for his philosophical development.[1] In response to this experience he wrote his first book *On the Form of the American Mind* in 1928. Voegelin became a lecturer in political science and sociology at the University of Vienna in 1929. His early works included *Race and State* (1933), *The Race Idea in Intellectual History* (1933), *The Authoritarian State* (1936), and *Political Religions* (1938),[2] which were exposés of the developing menace of National Socialism. Given the atmosphere of the time, an independent thinker criticizing the government's ideology could have faced lethal consequences. Because Voegelin realized that his days were numbered if he stayed in Europe, he and his wife immigrated via Switzerland to the United States in 1938, escaping from the clutches of the Gestapo with only a few hours to spare. If he had been captured and executed, the Nazis would have cut short the life of a man who turned out to be one of the most important thinkers of the twentieth century. Who knows how many other similar scholars who would have gone on to enrich the world through their teaching and writing were in fact

1. See Sandoz, *The Voegelinian Revolution*, 18–22.

2. I am listing the English titles of books he wrote in German.

killed by the Nazis? In the following years, he taught at Louisiana State University (1942–1958), the University of Munich (1958–1969), and Stanford University (1969–1985). Voegelin was a very prolific author throughout his life. The English edition of his complete works consists of thirty-four volumes.[3] This series includes his most influential works, *The New Science of Politics* (1952), *Order and History* (5 vols. 1956–1987), and *Anamnesis* (1966), as well as collections of essays, and his massive (posthumously published) work *History of Political Ideas* (8 vols. written in the early 1940s). Voegelin died in 1985. His intellectual legacy is being continued by the members of the Eric Voegelin Society, which meets in connection with the American Political Science Association annual conference.

Basic Characteristics of His Thought

Various labels could be used to describe Voegelin: political philosopher, intellectual historian, philosopher of religion, philosopher of consciousness, Platonic theologian. These labels give an indication of the breadth and depth of his concerns. He was immensely erudite, not only regarding Mediterranean and Western civilization, but also regarding Eastern civilizations such as China and India. His knowledge of languages rivaled that of many philologists. Themes from philosophy, biblical studies, theology, politics, and literature were woven together in his thinking into a rich tapestry.

Some scholars work primarily on questions and problems that have been framed by others; Voegelin shows the opposite tendency, in the sense that he forged his own path without confining himself to the limitations imposed by scholarly conventions. The Enlightenment's establishment of "methodological atheism" as a basic rule of social science is a case in point. Methodological atheism dictates that the scholar's own religious beliefs, or lack thereof, have no bearing on the scholarship that he or she produces. Voegelin saw this as an absurd approach that prevented intellectuals from grasping reality, because human beings exist in a dynamic tension "in between" materiality and the divine source of all life. If this basic aspect of existence is "bracketed" or ignored, reality is being falsified, not understood.

3. This series was initiated by Louisiana State University Press, and has been brought to completion by the University of Missouri Press.

The observation of Voegelin's independence from scholarly conventions and limitations needs to be balanced, however, by the idea that he saw himself as a profoundly unoriginal thinker. In fact, he considered "originality" to be a sign of sloppy and superficial thinking. "The test of truth, to put it pointedly, will be the lack of originality in the propositions" (CWEV, 12: 122). The task of philosophy, in his view, is to study the wisdom of the past (the Bible, Plato, Aristotle, Augustine, Aquinas, and so forth) so that one will be led into a deeper experience and understanding of reality. Through study of key philosophers, religious leaders, and canonical texts, one is able to rise up in intellectual stature, in contrast with the laziness and immaturity of one's culture. The idea that *truth is accumulative* forms the heart of Voegelin's method as a thinker. This concept was expressed well by T. S. Eliot: "Some one said: 'The dead writers are remote from us because we *know* so much more than they did.' Precisely, and they are that which we know."[4]

The aspect of Voegelin's writings that poses the greatest challenge for the reader is his use of (and sometimes invention of) a very difficult vocabulary. He uses terms such as *dogmatomachy*, *egophany*, *metaxy*, and *spoudaios*. These concepts play important roles in his message, so that the reader must grasp them or risk becoming lost in a dense forest. He came to the conclusion that he needed to employ terms such as these, not because he wanted to write only for other scholars, but because the philosophical vocabulary he had inherited was in many ways inadequate for describing reality. Human existence within history and between God and the material world is an extremely complex phenomenon, and Voegelin sought to interpret that reality in depth by redeploying key concepts from ancient Greek philosophy that had been forgotten, or by inventing new terms that describe more recently appearing phenomena.[5]

Some thinkers arrive at what they consider to be an adequate way of expressing themselves and then they maintain that form of expression virtually unchanged for the rest of their lives. Theologian Karl Barth, in contrast, wrote a commentary on Romans, and then rewrote it almost completely from scratch for the second edition because his thinking was evolving so rapidly. He did the same thing again when he set out

4. Eliot, *Sacred Wood*, 52.

5. Voegelinian glossaries are found in Federici, *Eric Voegelin*, and in CWEV 34.

to write his main work of systematic theology. Voegelin is an example of the latter style of thinker, who is always open to growth and change in his form of expression, even if that means abandoning projects and philosophical frameworks that he had been developing for several years. Voegelin wrote out the manuscript for a multi-volume *History of Political Ideas*, only to decide that his basic methodology needed to be altered to such an extent that his manuscript could not be published. He then began work on his magnum opus, *Order and History*, which grew out of his new insights. After writing three volumes, he once again reconceived his philosophical enterprise, so that he needed to stop and restart with a somewhat different orientation. In other words, Voegelin is an excellent example of a thinker who is continually developing and growing as he moves through time, in sharp contrast with a small-minded dogmatist who knows what he believes and doesn't want to hear anything different. (Small-minded dogmatists are sometimes religious and sometimes anti-religious.) Those readers who want to know more about these stops and starts in Voegelin's authorship are referred to Ellis Sandoz' biography, *The Voegelinian Revolution*, and also to Voegelin's own *Autobiographical Reflections* (CWEV 34).

Central Themes

A consideration of some of the main ideas and themes in Voegelin's thought will serve to introduce the reader to the substance of his message. The dominant theme in his writings is clearly *order and disorder in soul and society*. The right order of soul and society has a recognizable structure, which Voegelin describes with a four-part analysis. The elements of the structure are God, material nature, the human person, and society. The person exists in the middle of the other elements; we live in between God and nature, church and state, and so forth. The difficult task that faces us as human beings is maintaining a dynamic balance and tension among the elements as we exist in the middle of them. Glenn Hughes offers an excellent summary of Voegelin in these words: "The balance of consciousness, then, is psychological and existential equilibrium in full openness to the mystery of reality, honoring the truth of transcendence, while remaining committed to the search for truth and goodness in worldly existence."[6] There is a temptation, for example,

6. Hughes, "Balanced and Unbalanced Consciousness," 169.

when we become aware of God, to seek to flee from this fallen world and escape to the divine realm to be with God. The opposite temptation is atheistic rejection of God and transcendence. Those readers who are familiar with Kierkegaard's book *The Sickness unto Death* will recognize that Voegelin is offering a similar perspective, which was no doubt been influenced by his reading of Kierkegaard. *The Sickness unto Death* speaks of the human self as a synthesis of polar elements: the infinite and the finite, the eternal and the temporal, freedom and necessity; the book also describes various levels of human self-consciousness.[7] Voegelin's thought works with these elements, extending Kierkegaard's insights into a comprehensive interpretation of human consciousness, politics, and history.

The structural elements of reality (God, nature, the person, society) are permanent features of human life. They were present in the ancient world, just as they are now. The difference between then and now is the phenomenon of *compactness* vs. *differentiation*. In the ancient world, human consciousness tended to be compact, meaning that the divine was not distinguished from nature and the person was not distinguished from society. Human history, under the impact of philosophical and theological insights, has seen a clearer differentiation of the elements. The problem that faces us as "modern" persons is finding the appropriate pathway for reintegration of the elements.

When human beings fail to maintain a dynamic tension between the elements of reality, the result is the many forms of disorder in soul and society. The religious tradition understands this disorder under the headings of *fallenness* and *sin*. If these terms are not used, something else must replace them such as "unfortunate behavior."[8] Voegelin is on a quest to find the source of this disorder, and the source of our typical blindness to it and inability to escape from it.

One possible answer to the problem of disorder is *Gnosticism*. This view, which began in the ancient world and has been reawakened at various points in time up to the present, maintains that the material world is inherently fallen and corrupt. The material world cannot be transformed or redeemed, since it comes from a different source than

7. See Grøn, "Human Synthesis."

8. Once, I was speaking with a self-described atheist, who objected to my use of the word "sin." I asked him what word he would use to describe the actions of Hitler, and after reflecting, he offered this elegant phrase.

that which is good and holy. To put it bluntly: the material world of nature comes from Satan, and if one hopes to commune with God one must find a way to escape from materiality. Gnosticism is the broad term that is used to indicate the many different pathways human beings have invented in their quest to escape from the material world to some "higher" world of spirituality and truth.

In Voegelin's view, Gnosticism is not simply of antiquarian interest as a bizarre phenomenon in the ancient world. Rather, it is at the heart of the modern world as well, and has been dominating the political scene in very subtle ways. Voegelin thus engages in a very forceful *critique of modern thought forms*. The thought patterns under examination are those forms of self-understanding and those political ideologies of the past few centuries that begin by turning away from the central truths of Judeo-Christian revelation and from the philosophical insights of Plato and Aristotle, in favor of the shrunken self's egocentric misconstrual of reality:

> Only in recent years have I developed the concept of the "egophanic revolt," in order to designate the concentration on the epiphany of the ego as the fundamental experience that eclipses the epiphany of God in the structure of Classic and Christian consciousness . . . the term egophanic revolt, distinguishing this experience of the exuberant ego from the experience of the theophanic constitution of humanity, is the best I can do terminologically at present. (CWEV 34:94)

Gnosticism is a rejection of reality, both the reality of the material world, and also the reality of the tradition of wisdom we have been given by earlier generations of human beings. Because Gnostics exist in a fundamental revolt against reality, they must invent a "second reality" in which they can live. That is, they invent a fantasy world where the human will is able to rearrange the elements of reality. Both Marxism and Naziism are forms of Gnosticism that seek to do precisely this. The idea of escaping *from* the material world has been transformed into an escape *within* the world into a new form of existence. In both of these political movements, a "spiritual" elite defines good and evil in starkly dualistic terms, and understands its proper role to be the elimination of the "evil" human beings so that a new society can be invented. A recognition of human limitations, fallibility, and the duty to treat other people ethically is rejected in favor of an apocalyptic vision of the purification of society through an orgiastic festival of violence. Thus the modern forms of Gnosticism express themselves as what Voegelin calls *ideologies of murder*:

> A further reason for my hatred of . . . ideologies is quite a primitive one. I have an aversion to killing people for the fun of it. What the fun is, I did not quite understand at the time, but in the intervening years the ample exploration of revolutionary consciousness has cast some light on this matter.
>
> The fun consists in gaining a pseudo-identity through asserting one's power, optimally by killing somebody—a pseudo-identity that serves as a substitute for the human self that has been lost. (CWEV, 34:74–75)

The intellectual groundwork for these ideologies was laid in the nineteenth century by Hegel, Marx, and Nietzsche, who are spiritually diseased personalities subjected by Voegelin to a withering critique.[9]

But this *descent into the abyss*, as Voegelin calls it,[10] which was led by intellectual midgets posing as giants, did not occur without resistance from other thinkers who had allowed themselves to be shaped and sustained by the religious, philosophical, and moral traditions of the West. Voegelin shows that at any point in history human beings can live in openness to reality, instead of closing themselves off from it and inventing a Gnostic second reality. Such openness means that one lives as a human being who learns from the wisdom of the past, interacts constructively and ethically with one's fellow human beings, and responds to the *pull of the divine* to enter into the genuine life of the spirit:

> By spirit we understand the openness of man to the divine ground of his existence: by estrangement from the spirit, the closure and the revolt against the ground. Through spirit man actualizes his potential to partake of the divine. He rises thereby to the *imago Dei* which it is his destiny to be. Spirit in this classical sense of *nous*, is that which all men have in common.
>
> . . .
>
> Through the life of the spirit, which is common to all, the existence of man becomes existence in community. In the openness of the common spirit there develops the public life of so-

9. See "On Hegel: A Study in Sorcery," in CWEV, 12; *Science, Politics, and Gnosticism* in CWEV, 5 (Marx); and "Nietzsche, "The Crisis, and the War," in CWEV, 10.

10. See Voegelin, *Hitler and the Germans* CWEV, 31.

> ciety. He, however, who closes himself against what is common, or who revolts against it, removes himself from the public life of human community. He becomes thereby a private man, or in the language of Heraclitus, an *idiotes*.
>
> Now it is possible, however, and it occurs all the time, that the *idiotes*—that is, the man estranged from the spirit—becomes the socially dominant figure.[11] The public life of society is thus characterized not only by the spirit, but also through the possibility of estrangement from it. Between the extremes of the spiritually genuine public life and the disintegration of a society through the radical privatization of its members, lie the actual concrete societies with their complex field of tensions between spirit and estrangement. Every concrete society, therefore, has its own particular character of public life through which the genuineness or sickness of its spirit can be recognized. (CWEV, 12:7)

To live in openness to the pull of the divine, to God's summons to maturity as a human being, means that one is able to discover the pathway that leads toward order in the soul and in society, in stark contrast with the disorder that is the product of the Gnostic rejection of reality.

Voegelin sees *philosophy* and *revelation* as the two main sources of insight into order. By "philosophy" he understands primarily Plato and Aristotle, and those subsequent thinkers who have built upon them. By "revelation" he understands the Jewish and Christian scriptures, and the theological traditions that have arisen out of them. Voegelin describes philosophy and revelation as two different sources of *theophany*, as the means through which human beings can become conscious of the pull of the divine as the true source of order in the soul and in society.

The following passage effectively expresses Voegelin's mature reflections on the spiritual situation of human beings:

> Divine reality is being revealed to man in two fundamental modes of experience: in the experience of divine creativity in the cosmos and in the experience of divine ordering presence in the soul.
>
> The two modes are always structures in man's consciousness of divine reality, but they are not always conscious in the form of reflected knowledge. The experience is the area of reality where the revelatory appeal from the divine side meets with the questing response from the human side, and reflective medita-

11. When I read this line, I think of Adolf Hitler.

> tion on the response is preceded by millennia of less reflected response in the form of cosmological symbolization. Only late in history, when man becomes aware of himself, of his spirit and intellect, as an active partner in the cognition of divine reality, will the two modes be discerned and adequately symbolized. Only when the response becomes luminous to itself as a quest for the divine ground, and when the quest becomes an act of reflective questioning, will man find himself moving either in the direction of divine creativity towards a beginning of things, or in the direction of the ordering presence within his soul toward a divine Beyond as its source. . . .
>
> The symbols of the Beginning and the Beyond, thus, express the dynamics of the experience in all of its aspects. They articulate, first of all, the divine reality that draws man into the quest; they express furthermore the structure of consciousness in its questing tension toward the divine ground of things and of itself; and they finally bring into view the structure of reality that channels both the divine drawing and the human questing. This superb precision in articulating the structure of the experience has endowed the two symbols with their millennial durability ever since they were found in antiquity. (CWEV, 28:173–74)

This passage contains prose that is a bit difficult for the average reader, but its content can be made more broadly understood, which is my goal in this chapter. Voegelin is referring here to two of the three dimensions of life that will constitute the heart of my argument in this book. He is referring here to the vertical dimension, which is the axis constituted by God and nature, with human beings "in between." God is the Source, the Creator, the Beginning of things. He is also referring to the temporal trajectory of individual selfhood. Here, God is the one who calls us forward into greater maturity as human beings; God is the goal of our spiritual striving, the Beyond at the completion of life. The third dimension, which Voegelin is not developing in this particular passage, is the horizontal, social plane. He has a great deal to say about that dimension in other essays and books.[12]

12. His critiques of Naziism and Marxism as horizontal pathologies are found in the works I have already referred to. In later sections of this book I will describe René Girard's interpretation of the Holy Spirit as the Paraclete, the Defense Attorney. If Girard could revise this passage from Voegelin, he would likely speak of the Beginning, the Beyond, and the Paraclete.

Voegelin argues that there is a three-stage pattern that is observable in human history. The first stage is constituted by the genuine experiences of reality and God (theophanies) that are seen in the prophets and apostles and in the true philosophers. A second stage is seen when the writings of the first stage are turned into the basis for a rigid doctrinal system that is cut off from its experiential roots. The third stage emerges in the form of a skeptical critique of the second stage. Applied to Western history, the three stages can be thought of as follows: (1) the Bible, Plato, and Aristotle; (2) Christianity as a diseased cultural institution, e.g., the Crusades and the Wars of Religion; (3) Enlightenment critiques of Christianity.[13]

Voegelin's thought seeks to lead us toward a renewed experience of God; it seeks to bring us back into the first stage. This is the meaning of the Greek word *anamnesis*, as Voegelin is using it. *Anamnesis* means recollection, remembrance, recovery of what was lost. This concept has two aspects in Voegelin's message: (1) *anamnesis* in the sense of inhabiting truthfully the vertical axis, living expansively as a creature in between God and nature; and (2) *anamnesis* in the sense of accumulating the wisdom of the past, recovering the truths articulated by the ancient philosophers, prophets, and apostles. These are two sides of the same coin. This passage summarizes Voegelin's approach:

> The doctrinaire segmentation of history has found its climactic expression in the formula: "We are living in a post-Christian age." Every style, even the doctrinaire, has its beauties of perfection—and the philosopher cannot suppress his admiration for the neat trick of turning the "post-Christ" of the Christians into the "post-Christian" of the ideologues.
>
> Thanks to existential assent, the formula has become widely accepted in our society. Thinkers who otherwise rank above the level of ordinary intellectuals propound it with a serious, if sorrowful, face; and even theologians, who ought to know better, are softening under constant pressure and display a willingness to demythologize their dogma, to abandon the most charm-

13. See CWEV, 12:54–55, 74–80. Sam Harris's *End of Faith* is a recent example of this type of Enlightenment critique, though Harris's totalitarian implications render the Enlightenment credentials of the book very ambiguous. It is clear that he lacks the ability to distinguish between historically derailed forms of religion and the authentic spiritual experiences that lie at the beginning of religious traditions. David Hart's review of a book by Daniel Dennett is pertinent reading in relation to Harris as well. See Hart, "Daniel Dennett Hunts the Snark."

> ing miracles, to renounce the virgin birth, and glumly to admit that God is dead. The attitude is regrettable; for a truth whose symbols have become opaque and suspect cannot be saved by doctrinal concessions to the *Zeitgeist*, but only by a return to the reality of experience which originally has engendered the symbols. The return will engender its own exegesis and the exegetic language will make the older symbols translucent again. (CWEV, 12:73)

This passage serves well as an outline of the neo-orthodox theology of a thinker such as Karl Barth. Voegelin can very plausibly be described as a neo-orthodox philosopher. He has an attitude toward the past that is respectful yet critical. He realizes that truth is accumulative and his thought shows why this understanding constitutes the health of the human soul. He is a superb model of how a philosopher should live and work: resisting the moral illiteracy of one's age by being open to growth in understanding of reality and in concern for one's fellow human beings.

4

Mimesis: Introduction to René Girard

Life and Writings

René Girard was born in Avignon, France, in 1923.[1] He studied philosophy and medieval studies at two universities in France. He came to Indiana University in 1947 and earned a PhD in History in 1950. He taught French language and literature at Indiana until 1953. From 1953 to 1957 he taught at Bryn Mawr College, and from 1957 to 1971 at Johns Hopkins University. From 1971 to 1976 Girard occupied a position as a distinguished professor at the State University of New York at Buffalo. From 1976 to 1981 he taught again at Johns Hopkins, moving finally to Stanford University where he taught until retiring in 1995. Girard's formal studies were mostly in history, but his teaching and writing over the years gravitated toward literary criticism, anthropology, and religious studies.

In the late 1950s and early 1960s he researched and wrote his first two books, *Deceit, Desire, and the Novel* (1961), and *Resurrection from the Underground: Feodor Dostoevksy* (1963).[2] These books focused on mimetic desire as it is revealed in the works of certain modern novelists such as Cervantes, Flaubert, Stendahl, Dostoevsky, and Proust. During the 1960s he became interested in the phenomenon of violence in human culture, turning his attention to psychological and anthropological theories of violence, as well as the ancient Greek playwrights. This study resulted in the publication in 1972 of *Violence and the Sacred*, which

1. For an expanded account of Girard's life, see *The Girard Reader*, 1–6.

2. Girard's books are published in French and then translated into English by others. I am listing the titles of the English translations, with the date of their original publication (in French).

applied the concept of mimetic desire to the task of understanding the scapegoat mechanism in human history. In 1978 Girard published the transcripts of his conversations with two psychiatrists under the title *Things Hidden since the Foundation of the World*; this was the first work in which he argued that the gospels reveal the violent structure of human culture in a unique way. In the same year he brought out a collection of essays: *"To Double Business Bound": Essays on Literature, Mimesis, and Anthropology*. He published *The Scapegoat* in 1982, which further developed his theory of violence and his reading of the gospels. In 1985 he published *Job, the Victim of His People*, an interpretation of the biblical book of Job through the lens of the scapegoating theory. His next work was *A Theater of Envy: William Shakespeare*, published in 1991. In 1999 he published *I See Satan Fall Like Lightning*, which repeats and refines his often-stated theory of mimetic desire and scapegoating, and includes commentaries on Nietzsche and on the significance of "concern for victims" as a key feature of the modern world.

From this overview, we can see that Girard's thought is very wide-ranging and interdisciplinary. His ideas have attracted a large number of followers and respondents from various academic fields. In 1990 an association of scholars called the Colloquium on Violence and Religion was formed; it defined its mission as exploring the implications of Girard's thought in a variety of fields: literature, drama, religion, philosophy, sociology, psychology, law, criminology, economics, history, and so forth. COVR began the journal *Contagion* in 1994, and continues to hold regular conferences in North America and Europe. In 2005, Girard was elected to *L'Academie Francaise*, which is the highest honor bestowed on a French intellectual.

Outline of Girard's Theory of Society

Girard begins with the concept of mimetic desire. We human beings have a natural tendency to look to others as models of success. We think that by imitating others we deem to be successful, we will come to share in their greater fullness of being. We want to have what they have so that we can be as important as they are. This basic driving force in human affairs—mimetic desire—can be seen in the psychology of small children, in advertising, in romantic relationships, in fashion, in economics, and on and on. If you put two small children in a room that has an abundance of toys, what will happen? As soon as the question is asked, the answer is obvious. After a period of experimentation with various toys, one child will decide that the toy being held by the other is the best toy in the room and will try to take it away. A power struggle will develop for the possession of that particular toy, *even if there is another identical toy in the room*. This "primitive" scene from childhood is played out in a million subtle (and not so subtle) ways in the lives of adults; this playing out *is* human culture, from Girard's point of view.

The next key step in Girard's theory is the observation that "I suffer from your attractiveness."[3] Social relations are a kind of gravitational field that pulls us into an orbit that creates conflict. If I am copying the desires of others, wanting to possess what they possess, then by definition I will create a rivalry with those others for the possession of those things. And if those others become defensive in response to my rivalrous intentions, then we have the recipe for a war of all against all for possession of the idols of our desire. How does human society prevent itself from degenerating into a chaos of violence driven by envy? As Caiaphas said: "You do not understand that it is better for you to have one man die for the people than to have the whole nation destroyed" (John 11:50). Channeling violence toward a scapegoat is society's solution to the problem of chaos, according to Girard's theory. Killing a scapegoat, or attacking a minority group within society, provides an outlet valve for the build up of hatreds, resentments, and violent impulses that are generated by mimetic desire. Killing the scapegoat is a cathartic event that creates a new sense of social unanimity that did not exist before. Sacrifice becomes salvific for the society, and it becomes the cornerstone of both religion and culture.

The sacrificial act of scapegoating is remembered in a disguised form in the myths by which a culture interprets reality. Girard extensively develops this point by analyzing many ancient cultures, creation myths, religious belief systems, etc. It needs to be emphasized that his theory is a critique of a particular modern notion, the idea that "religion causes violence." To a great extent, what we call the Enlightenment happened because of the power of this mistaken idea.[4] In the wake of the

3. At a Colloquium on Violence and Religion conference, I overheard someone using this phrase, but I am not sure to whom it should be attributed. As far as I know it is not a phrase from Girard's writings, but a gloss on them.

4. "The myth of early modern 'religious wars' from which the modern state has saved

post-Reformation wars of religion, it was asserted by skeptical critics of faith that religion causes violence by inflaming people's passions and giving them an absolute belief in their own righteousness. Girard turns the idea that "religion causes violence" on its head by *showing* (not simply asserting) that *violence causes religion*. Human beings are violent for reasons that can be understood psychologically, and what we call mythology or religion arises in the wake of actual events of violence that meet psychological needs. If a person wants to find a cannon within the canon, if they want to find religious justifications for their violence, they will, but this tells us more about the (mis)interpreter of the scriptures than it does about the genuine theological message of the scriptures.

Human cultures answer the threat of a war of all against all through the scapegoat mechanism. But this answer is false, because the problem should not exist in the first place. The mimetic desire at the root of the social system is itself a falling away from God; Girard calls it an "ontological sickness" (DDN, 238–39). In other words, deceit becomes essential to society as it must not become aware of its sickness and of the consequent destruction of arbitrary scapegoats. Society must lie to itself about its foundation, adopt hypocrisy as its basic mode of operation, and keep itself in the dark about what is really happening. This is precisely what happened in Western history, as the peaceful gospel of Jesus became twisted into the violence of the Crusades, the Inquisition, and anti-Semitic pogroms:

> Now it is the Christians who say: *If we had lived in the days of our Jewish fathers, we would not have taken part with them in shedding the blood of Jesus*. If the people whom Jesus addresses and who do not listen to him fulfill the measure of their fathers, then the Christians who believe themselves justified in denouncing these same people in order to exculpate themselves are fulfilling a measure that is already full to overflowing. They claim to be governed by the text that reveals the process of misunderstanding, and yet they repeat that misunderstanding. With their eyes fixed on the text, they do once again what the text condemns. (TH, 175)

---

us is historically untrue. The rise of the modern secular state is a historically contingent event that has produced more, not less, violence. It has done so not by secularizing politics, but by supplanting the imagination of the body of Christ with a heretical theology of salvation through the state." See Cavanaugh, *Theopolitical Imagination*, 5.

> Thanks to the sacrificial reading it has been possible for what we call Christendom to exist for fifteen or twenty centuries; that is to say, a culture has existed that is based, like all cultures (at least up to a certain point) on the mythological forms engendered by the founding mechanism. Paradoxically, in the sacrificial reading the Christian text itself provides the basis. Humankind relies upon a misunderstanding of the text that explicitly reveals the founding mechanism to re-establish cultural forms which remain sacrificial and to engender a society that, by virtue of this misunderstanding, takes its place in the sequence of all other cultures, still clinging to the sacrificial vision that the Gospel rejects. (TH, 181)

This strand of Girard's thought, which criticizes historical Christianity for betraying the Bible's insights, is very similar to Kierkegaard's critique of "Christendom as an illusion," which makes it necessary to "reintroduce Christianity into Christendom" (PV, 41–44, 123–24).

Girard's vision of human culture leads beyond the narrowness of secular social science to a broader theological anthropology. Girard clearly states that we can only articulate this understanding of violence as the foundation of human culture because our eyes have been opened up by the Bible. It is the cumulative effect of divine revelation in the Jewish and Christian scriptures that has exposed the ontological sickness of mimetic desire and the scapegoating mechanism:

> Modern interpreters certainly see that everything in the Kingdom of God comes down to the project of ridding men of violence. But because they conceive of violence in the wrong way, they do not appreciate the rigorous objectivity of the methods which Jesus advocates. People imagine either that violence is no more than a kind of parasite, which the appropriate safeguards can easily eliminate or that it is an ineradicable trait of human nature, an instinct or fatal tendency that it is fruitless to fight.
>
> But the Gospels tell quite a different story. Jesus invites all men to devote themselves to the project of getting rid of violence, a project conceived with reference to the true nature of violence, taking into account the illusions it fosters, the methods by which it gains ground, and all the laws that we have verified over the course of these discussions.
>
> Violence is the enslavement of a pervasive lie; it imposes upon men a falsified vision not only of God but also of everything else. And that is indeed why it is a closed kingdom.

> Escaping from violence is escaping from this kingdom into another kingdom, whose existence the majority of people do not even suspect. This is the Kingdom of love, which is also the domain of the true God, the Father of Jesus, of whom the prisoners of violence cannot even conceive. (TH, 197)

Girard's thought is primarily critique of human psychopathology, but here and there in his writings he provides glimpses such as this of his positive vision.

The high point of revelation is the Gospels' depiction of the crucifixion of Christ, which tears the mask off of culture's insistence that it is in the right when it executes people. The Gospels expose this lie by showing that Christ is innocent and that those who are killing him are in the wrong.[5] In that revelation God triumphs and Satan is defeated. Girard understands Satan to be that principle in human psychology and culture that cries out for bloodshed, for violence, for revenge, for destruction. Satan is the Accuser, the prosecuting attorney; his arch enemy is the Holy Spirit, as Girard explains:

> What is this power that triumphs over mimetic violence? The Gospels respond that it is the Spirit of God, the third person of the Trinity, the Holy Spirit. The Spirit takes charge of everything. It would be false, for example, to say the disciples "regained possession of themselves": it is the Spirit of God that possesses them and does not let them go.
>
> In the Gospel of John the name given to this Spirit admirably describes the power that tears the disciples away from this all-powerful contagion: the Paraclete. I have commented on this term in other essays, but its importance for what I am doing in this book is so great that I must return to it. The principal meaning of *parakletos* is "lawyer for the defense," "defender of the accused." In place of looking for paraphrases and loopholes to avoid this translation, we should prefer it to all others and marvel at its relevance. We should take with utmost seriousness the idea that the Spirit enlightens the persecutors concerning their acts of persecution. The Spirit discloses to individuals the literal truth of what Jesus said during his crucifixion: "They don't know what they are doing." We should also think of the God whom Job calls "my defender."

5. An overview of Girard's thought in relation to the Bible is provided by Williams in *The Bible, Violence, and the Sacred.*

> The birth of Christianity is a victory of the Paraclete over his opposite, Satan, whose name originally means "accuser before a tribunal," that is, the one responsible for proving the guilt of the defendants. That is one of the reasons why the Gospels hold Satan responsible for all mythology. The Passion accounts are attributed to the spiritual power that defends victims unjustly accused. This corresponds marvelously to the human content of the revelation, to the extent that violent contagion permits it to be understood.
>
> The anthropological revelation is not prejudicial to the theological revelation or in competition with it. It is inseparable from it. This union of the two is demanded by the dogma of the Incarnation, the mystery of the double nature of Jesus Christ, divine and human. The "mimetic" reading permits a better realization of this union. (ISS, 189–90)

Girard's theory arises out of his perception that conventional literary criticism and social science are limited in their explanatory power. They are a bit dull-witted at times. To be brought into a more lively engagement with the reality of human psychology and culture, these disciplines need to be opened up to a broader horizon of thought that is provided by the scriptures and by the refraction of scriptural insights in authors such as Shakespeare and Dostoevsky. In other words, Girard sees himself as a philosophical anthropologist who is wrestling with the inadequate understanding of human beings that is the product of the Enlightenment. He is trying to confront secular social science and to bring it, kicking and screaming, to the place where it is forced to comprehend human beings in the light of the crucifixion of Christ. He does this not simply by preaching at secular social science, but by diving into it deeply and revealing its inadequacies from within. He shows that the phenomenon of social science itself, the effort by human beings to understand themselves, has been made possible by the way the scriptural tradition has subtly undermined sacrificial thinking over the course of many centuries:

> . . . we can no longer believe that it is we who are reading the Gospels in the light of an ethnological, modern revelation which is truly primary. We have to reverse the order. It is still the great Judaeo-Christian spirit that is doing the reading. All that appears in ethnology, appears in the light of a continuing revelation, an immense process of historical work that enables us little

> by little to catch up with texts that are, in effect, already quite explicit, though not for the kind of people that we are—who *have eyes and see not, ears and hear not.* (TH, 177)

If the human race were still completely dominated by the falsity of the scapegoat mechanism, there could be no such thing as social science. In Girard's words:

> The invention of science is not the reason that there are no longer witch-hunts, but the fact that there are no longer witch-hunts is the reason that science has been invented. The scientific spirit, like the spirit of enterprise in an economy, is a by-product of the profound action of the Gospel text. (TS, 204–5)

It is clear that *mimesis*, which is a horizontal, sociological concept, is at the heart of Girard's message. This is his *emphasis*, in contrast with Kierkegaard's emphasis on selfhood, and Voegelin's emphasis on the vertical axis of God and nature.[6] Girard presents his reader with the profound question: who is your model? Are you mimicking models provided by your (violent) culture? Or are you allowing God to transform you by taking Christ as your model?

~

To recap the ground we have covered, first we discussed the concept of the three dimensions of reality; and then we considered summaries of Kierkegaard, Voegelin, and Girard. These authors are aware of all three dimensions, but it is still accurate to note that they tend to emphasize the selfhood (SK), vertical (EV), and horizontal (RG) dimensions respectively. What happens when we interweave Kierkegaard's *askesis*, Voegelin's *anamnesis*, and Girard's *mimesis*? This is our topic in part 2. There I will argue that the deepest root of violence is the failure of human beings to integrate the dimensions successfully; a correlative picture of human spiritual health will also be presented, as the holistic expansion of human life through inhabiting all of the dimensions in a rich and complex way. This dual understanding of sin and salvation is an updated form of the medieval concepts of *exitus* (leaving) and *redi-*

6. Girard says that he does not write as a theologian, but we have seen in this summary how God's revelation of scapegoating plays a key role in his thought. Girard focuses on interdividuality (the horizontal), but with an awareness that the development of genuine individuality (selfhood) is the goal. On this point, see TH, 199.

tus (returning), the pathway of the human spirit as it becomes alienated from and comes back to God the Creator.

PART TWO

Perichoresis

The doctrine of the Trinity, taken literally, has no practical relevance at all, even if we think we understand it; and it is even more clearly irrelevant if we realize that it transcends all our concepts. Whether we are to worship three or ten persons in the Divinity makes no difference. . . . The same holds true of the doctrine that one person of the Godhead became man. For if we think of this God-man, not as the Idea of humanity in its full moral perfection, present in God from eternity and beloved by Him, but as the Divinity "dwelling incarnate" in a real man and working as a second nature in him, then we can draw nothing practical from this mystery: since we cannot require ourselves to rival a God, we cannot take him as an example.

—Immanuel Kant, *The Conflict of the Faculties*, 65–67

I believe that man exists and moves and has his being in God; that his fundamental relation is to God. That is the starting point, not the conclusion.

—H. Richard Niebuhr, *The Responsible Self*, 44

Modern thought that may appear to be quite post-Christian or at least postmetaphysical or postmoral may actually have trinitarian elements at the deepest levels.

—Max Stackhouse, "The Trinity as Public Theology," 181–82

Time which is torn apart into past, present and future is time which is diseased, and it does an injury to human existence.

—Nicolai Berdyaev, *Slavery and Freedom*, 258

. . . our present world can finally only be understood as a perversion of the New Testament.

—Ivan Illich, *The Rivers North of the Future*, 169

Christianity teaches that Jesus is the supremely consequential person for all; modern humanism insists that each of us, as individuals, is sufficient for ourselves.

—R. R. Reno, *Redemptive Change*, 197

Sin is evasion of time.

—Glenn Tinder, *The Fabric of Hope*, 220

Violence must be done to the self before it can be done to others.

—Michael Ignatieff, *The Warrior's Honor*, 54

Evil cannot be fought frontally, but can only be overcome by the slow development of a true vision of reality.

—Raymund Schwager, *Banished from Eden*, 160

Christ is the one who is himself the truest "rebel," entering human history with a divine disregard for its internal economies, disrupting it in fact at the deepest level by sowing freedom with almost profligate abandon among creatures who—with very few exceptions—are incapable of receiving it.

—David Hart, *The Doors of the Sea*, 43

As you, Father, are in me and I am in you, may they also be in us.

—John 17:21

The whole destiny of humanity is christological.

—Olivier Clément, *On Human Being*, 40

Christ came to make a new world. He came into the world to regenerate it in Himself, to make a new beginning, to be the beginning of the creation of God, to gather together in one, and recapitulate all things in Himself.

—John Henry Newman, "The Three Offices of Christ"

. . . in him all his Father shon
Substantially express'd, and in his face
Divine compassion visibly appeerd,
Love without end, and without measure Grace,
Which uttering thus he to his Father spake.

—John Milton, *Paradise Lost*, Book III

5

Theses on Trinitarian Anthropology and Violence

We Are Able to See the Dimensions Displayed in Human Behavior Patterns

LET US SUPPOSE, FOR THE SAKE OF DISCUSSION, THAT HUMAN BEINGS have difficulty inhabiting the three dimensions of reality in an expansive and balanced way, that we often focus our energies on one dimension to the relative exclusion of the others. This lack of balance twists and warps the structure of human life in its various dimensions. The result is three master types that can be described as the God-centered personality (vertical), the Self-centered personality (temporal), and the Society-centered personality (horizontal).

I will use the term *fundamentalism* as a label for the God-centered personality type. This pattern of thinking and living will place the emphasis on living in response to what it perceives as the will of God. It will have an understanding of God that is based on reading a sacred scripture. God and God's Word decisively shape how human selfhood and society are evaluated. The Truth is understood to come from above, from on high. The word "absolute" is often attached as an adjective: "We believers adhere to the Absolute Truth in an age of relativism."[1] The highest virtue is obedience to divine directives. This emphasis on the upper half of the vertical axis contrasts with deep suspicion regarding the lower half of the vertical axis, the domain of nature as it is studied

1. For an expansion of this topic, see Charles Kimball, *When Religion Becomes Evil*, chapter 2. The entire book is relevant as an analysis of fundamentalism. Similar overviews, focusing on the Muslim world, have been provided by Abdelwahab Meddeb in *The Malady of Islam* and by Khaled Abou El Fadl in *The Great Theft: Wrestling Islam from the Extremists.*

by the natural sciences. The idea of evolution is obviously very disturbing for fundamentalism. Modern science, with its *a posteriori* method of investigating evidence, is threatening to scriptural inerrancy's *a priori* method of logical assumptions that are believed before any evidence is considered. This leads to the development of what Eric Voegelin calls a "dogmatomachy," a war of ideologies between fundamentalists and their rival siblings the atheistic scientists (such as Richard Dawkins and his ilk). This war brings the vertical axis into our field of vision very clearly.

The person living in this pattern will typically inhabit the temporal trajectory of selfhood by placing the emphasis on *the past*, which is seen as a Golden Age when the scriptures were revealed. In contrast, the present, modernity, is a troublesome time, which is characterized mainly by apostasy from the Truth that has been revealed. The future is usually perceived by this personality type in one of two ways, both of which are apocalyptic. There may be (1) a vision of Armageddon, when the world as we know it goes up in flames, to be replaced by a new world that comes down from heaven; or (2) a vision of a remaking of this world through the political ascendancy of the people of faith (a theocracy). Both of these possibilities interpret the social, horizontal plane along lines that are sharply dualistic. Humanity is divided into two camps: the children of light and the children of darkness. The fundamentalist will, of course, always see him or herself as being on the side of the Good people, who are involved in cosmic conflict with the Evil people.[2] The Good will win the conflict in the end, because they are the true servants of the Almighty God. This apocalyptic thought pattern is expressed effectively in the "Left Behind" novels (which have sold millions of copies).

2. An excellent example of this type of thinking is seen in MacArthur, *Terrorism, Jihad, and the Bible.*

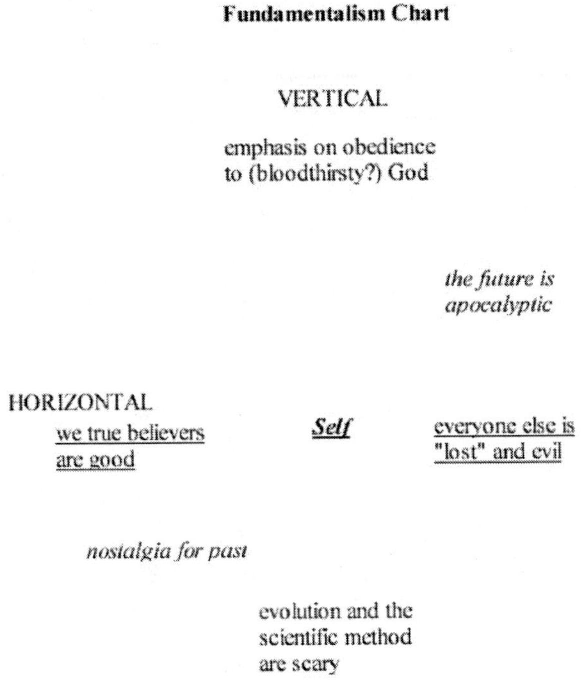

For those who inhabit another pattern of thought and life, which I will call *modernist individualism* or *aestheticism*, the most important thing is their own existence in the present moment. For them, every moment in time is "Me Time." Their primary concern is for themselves; they tend to use other people as means to their own ends. Living within the modern world suits the individualists well, because modernity is their Golden Age. More personal space and "freedom" are available to them now than have been in most ages in the past. Individualistic aesthetes are usually secularists, in the sense that they are allergic to "organized religion," though it may be the case that some form of disorganized religion suits their "spiritual needs." The idealized connection with God, that forms the core of fundamentalism, is cut off, to be replaced by the *self that relates itself to itself and in relating itself to itself relates itself to itself.* While the fundamentalist received truth from a sacred scripture, the concept of truth is interpreted pragmatically by the individualist as "whatever works for me" or "whatever I feel like believing at the present moment in time." The modern university and various forms of media such as magazines, television, and movies have been very effective conduits for the spread of individualistic aestheticism throughout Western culture.

The main element of this personality type is an individualistic focus on the self. Community, in the form of "religion" is seen as oppressive by forcing the individual to conform to restrictive moral codes and bizarre dogmas from past centuries. The past is identified with backwardness, ignorance, repression, intolerance, superstition, oppression, etc. All of this needs to be *left behind*, which is the liberal form of apocalyptic thinking. The only scenario that constitutes a bright future for the modern individualist is one in which more and more people become modern individualists by abandoning their superstitions and hang-ups. Community, in the form of the "state," is also a menacing threat in that it may take away the "rights" and "freedoms" that are so cherished by the individualists. Of course, the philosophical incoherence that results from cutting oneself off from transcendence and from the whole human past means that one is not able to articulate why human beings should have "rights" and "freedoms" at all,[3] but that minor point does not trouble the modern individualist. As long as one keeps telling oneself that "individual autonomy" is the highest value, then eventually one may believe that the concept makes sense.[4]

The individualist may seem to be non-religious, but this is an illusion, in that the Self has now become the idol for itself. In the words of Eric Voegelin, the "epiphany" of God has been replaced by "egophany."[5] The human Ego is now the center of meaning and value in the universe. The vertical dimension used to mean that the self was underneath the

3. For an expansion of this point, see G. P. Grant, *English-Speaking Justice*.

4. My comments here are obviously sketchy and simplistic. For a more sophisticated analysis of modern thought, see Manent's *City of Man*: "One is tempted to say that with Kant's moral philosophy, modern man has achieved clarity on what he had been seeking since the beginning of the modern movement. At last he can think what until that time he could only will: he can now think that he is neither a creature of God nor a part of Nature, that he is in short born of himself, the child of his own liberty." (189).

5. ". . . in the state of perfect self-reflection (Hegel) God is dead (de Sade, Hegel), and if he is not dead enough he must be murdered (Nietzsche), so that the egophanic God-man or superman (Feuerbach, Marx, Nietzsche) can establish the final realm of freedom in history. A radically egophanic 'history' is constructed with the intent of leaving no room for theophanic experiences and their symbolization." Voegelin, *Order and History, IV* (CWEV, 17:327).

reign of God; now that God is out of the picture, the self rises up in stature in its own eyes to fill the vacuum of sovereignty. Instead of God having the power of life and death, now it is the autonomous Ego that is all-powerful in deciding who lives. The individualistic suspicion of community indicates a contraction of human life into a very small box. Within the trajectory of time, the focus on the present, cut off from the past and the future,[6] combines with this contraction on the horizontal plane to replace dimensional complexity with a vision of the human person as a dot. Thomas Paine put it best: "My own mind is my own church."

Individualism Chart

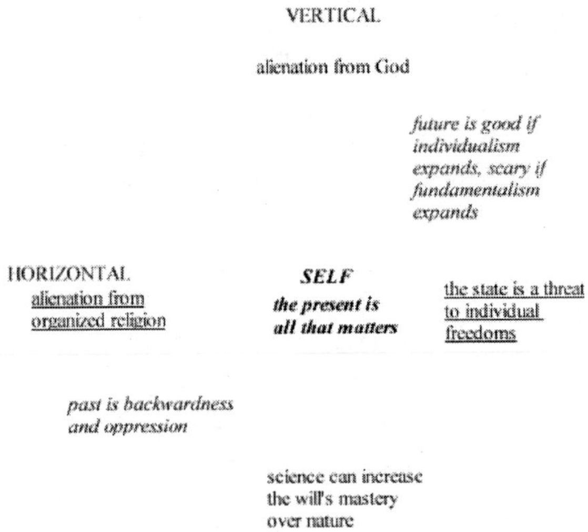

The society-centered or horizontal personality is seen in *political utopianism*, which in many ways is a mirror image of nostalgic fundamentalism. We can summarize utopianism by saying that it agrees with individualism that the past of the human race should be seen in basically negative terms, while it puts forward a vision of a socially engineered Golden Age in the future. The past represents religious superstition and economic oppression; "we revolutionaries," on the other hand, are able to understand the truth because we are "modern" people who

6. I have in mind here those arguments concerning abortion that assume that the future trajectory of the fetus has no moral relevance.

can envision a new world that we can make through our own efforts. The truth has come to birth for the first time in our thinking, and this truth is not based on learning anything substantive from history other than its errors.

From the point of view of the utopian, the fundamentalist is a hopelessly ignorant person who uses religion to keep people in a state of slavery and degradation by promising them rewards in the afterlife. "Religion is the opiate of the people," said Marx. The modern individualists are hardly any better, because even though they have escaped from dogmatic religion they are too selfish to see the need for a restructuring of society so that all people may enjoy the benefits that the elite take for granted. Their focus on themselves and the present moment in time is too narrow. In order for "autonomy" to be more than just a luxury for the rich, there must be a revolution that uses violence to remake society from the top down so that equality will replace the inequalities that result from free market economics. There must be a temporary tyranny of the leader of the revolution in order to bring an end, once and for all, to all forms of tyranny.

While the fundamentalist tries to revive a dead past, and the individualist seeks to maintain a self-centered present, the utopian is clearly pouring his or her energies into dreaming up a different future. "Liberation" is the new mantra, replacing the fundamentalist's "obedience" and the individualist's "autonomy." The state, if it is captured by the revolutionaries, becomes a positive value once again, in an interesting echo of the fundamentalist's fleeting dream of theocracy.

The utopian impulse in the modern world has a tendency to reduce the complexity of human consciousness for the purpose of gaining political control over the future. Our history books recount this story in depressing detail. The ideology claims that a new world order of justice is being fashioned, yet to the extent that this order is shaped by the eclipse of God and the rejection of the wisdom embodied in traditions of faith, it is not actually just at all. If one no longer respects the dignity of human lives and considers them expendable, then a pall is cast over everyone who survives the revolutionary apocalypse and has the good fortune to live in this new order of "justice."

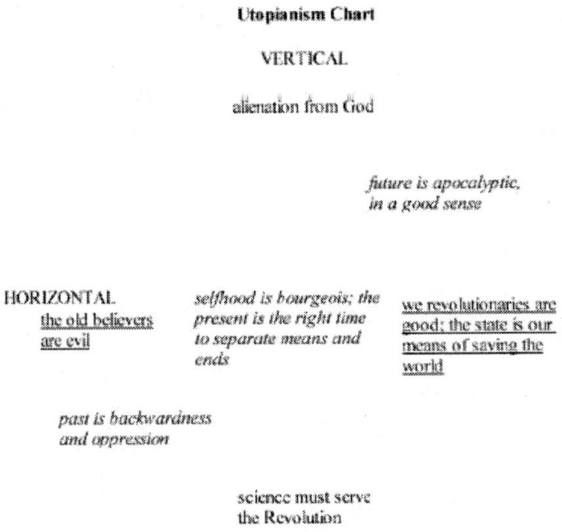

Individualistic aestheticism and utopianism are in agreement that the dead weight of the past is something you need to grow out of. The past is something you have to escape from like a snake has to shed its skin as it grows. Glenn Hughes describes the tendency of some people to have a view of history ". . . where the human past is seen primarily as a long passage through blindness and folly from which we have only recently begun to emerge, and our cultural heritage felt to be an imposition of authority from which we must struggle to liberate ourselves."[7] In other words, there is a great advantage to being born later in history, because you have the ability to participate in this awareness of the newly born truth that people in the past didn't have. But this perspective is simply another form of narrow arrogance in which the modern Self places itself in a position of power so that it may dominate reality.

Unbalanced Forms of Consciousness Can Be Understood and Critiqued By Persons Whose Consciousness Is Attuned to the Process of Human Maturing

In the previous section the portraits of personality types were generalized to such an extent that they bordered on being caricatures. In this

7. Hughes, *Transcendence and History*, 218.

section I will make the analysis a bit more concrete by referring to particular individuals and patterns of thought. I will also draw on authors who have a higher level of spiritual maturity and philosophical comprehension that enables them to see through the spiritual derailment that characterizes the unbalanced personality types.

Osama bin Laden and the 9/11 hijackers are examples of the fundamentalist (vertical) personality type. In 1998, Osama bin Laden and other Islamist leaders issued a fatwa that included statements such as these:

> The ruling to kill the Americans and their allies—civilians and military—is an individual duty for every Muslim who can do it in any country in which it is possible to do it. . . . We—with God's help—call on every Muslim who believes in God and wishes to be rewarded to comply with God's order to kill the Americans and plunder their money wherever and whenever they find it. We also call on Muslim religious scholars, leaders, youths, and soldiers to launch the raid on Satan's U.S. troops and the devil's supporters allying with them, and to displace those who are behind them so that they may learn a lesson. . . . Almighty God also says "O ye who believe, what is the matter with you, that when ye are asked to go forth in the cause of God, ye cling so heavily to the earth! Do ye prefer the life of this world to the hereafter? But little is the comfort of this life, as compared with the hereafter. Unless ye go forth, He will punish you with a grievous penalty, and put others in your place; but Him ye would not harm in the least. For God hath power over all things."[8]

This statement paints a picture of God that is delineated in clear terms: God is almighty; God will humiliate those infidels who are currently humiliating the true followers of God; it can be clearly known that God has ordered the killing of Americans; it can be clearly known that America is serving Satan, God's arch enemy. The faithful and zealous follower of this God believes that he is commanded by God to kill all those people who are viewed by the follower as infidels who are not true worshippers of God. Civilians may be killed in these efforts, though the preferred targets are those non-Muslim soldiers and their leaders who are viewed as having declared war on God, his messenger, and Muslims. The faithful followers of God are acting *defensively* in response to the

8. To find the full text, do an Internet search for a phrase from the selection I have presented.

terrorist acts of the Americans. Those who carry out these killings will be rewarded by God. If a Muslim who is able to carry out these killings does not do so, he will be punished by God.

In their own eyes, Osama bin Laden and his followers are the "good guys" and Americans are the "bad guys." This observation may appear obvious and banal, but how often do we reflect on its meaning? Consider *The Lord of the Rings*, for example. Its basic plot depicts a battle between the "good guys" (humans, hobbits, Gandalf, dwarves, and elves), and the "bad guys" (orcs, Saruman, Sauron). From the perspective of the 9/11 hijackers, they formed a "fellowship of the ring" to attack the Great Satan, the United States. They succeeded in bringing down two towers, which is parallel to Frodo making it into Mount Doom to destroy the Ring. If you compare the cinematic image of Sauron's Tower crumbling after the Ring is destroyed with images of the Twin Towers in New York collapsing, the effect is chilling. Of course, I am not suggesting that the 9/11 hijackers were "good guys" because this analogy can be drawn. I am suggesting that a way of thinking that divides the world simplistically into good and evil people is the problem, not the solution. Unfortunately, Tolkien's basic plot mirrors this simplistic way of thinking rather than challenging it. In this sense, Middle Earth is a pre-Christian vision. Where Christianity has had a decisive impact, awareness of the sinfulness of *all* human beings breaks down simplistic self-righteous dichotomies.

The letter found in the luggage of 9/11 hijacker Mohammed Atta is noteworthy.[9] Instead of quoting from the letter itself, I will draw on psychologist Ruth Stein, who has written articles that pinpoint precisely the psychopathology that was at work in the 9/11 hijackers as a warped relation to God and the vertical dimension of reality.

> The letter to the terrorists does not speak of hatred. It is past hatred. Absurdly and perversely, it is about love. It is about love of God. We can sense the confident intimacy of a son close to his father and the seeking of a love that is given as promised and no longer withheld. . . .
>
> The thought that there might be a root affinity between the theme of a son's love to his divine father and the underlying theme of the letter feels quite unpleasant. Do these motifs—of religious devotion and intimate communion and of using "God"

9. The text of the letter is reprinted in Lincoln, *Holy Terrors*, 93–98.

> to inflict mass killing and destruction—spring from the same psychic source? . . . Is there any similarity between the father of freedom and creativity, and the father who loves those who kill his enemies, and chooses those killers as his accepted sons? In both cases, the "father" not only dispenses empowerment and inspiration, he also imparts a sense of joy and fulfillment, the joy of deliverance from too enclosing a life and the opportunity to identify with ideals. . . .
>
> We also get the sense that such love, rather than expressing itself on a "horizontal axis" of compassion, nurturance, attachment, and the like, runs along a "vertical" axis of self-worth and unworth, which spans affects such as shame, humiliation, degradation, pity, awe, and veneration. A first step in understanding this affective syntax is to consider the blend of contempt and "love" found in the most blood-curdling sentence in the letter: "*You must not discomfort your animal during the slaughter*." This phrase is well beyond anger or hatred. It is the utmost in disparagement. . . .
>
> . . . a certain "God" has taken over and is monopolizing the psyche, and He now commands the would-be terrorist to kill the "infidel" part, so that He, God, will be content. The terrorist feels that God is pleased when his sons/followers annihilate His enemies. *But this is precisely why the terrorist loves God: because God allows, wants, sanctifies, the killing of the "bad part"* and, in addition, allows, desires, and sanctifies the orgiastic pleasure of disinhibited murdering and destruction. God is loved both for His licensing the ecstatic killing and for His offering a solution to the conflict-torn psyche at war with itself and with the complexity of life. . . .[10]

These passages from another article by Ruth Stein broaden the analysis to the topic of fundamentalism:

> Verticalization of difference engenders vertical desire. Vertical desire is the mystical longing for merger with the idealized other who requires abjection. On this view, the starkly opposing terms and polarizations with which fundamentalist thinking is suffused come to assume positions of higher and lower on a vertical axis. Since such binary oppositions, as we know, always result in inscribing inequality, *fundamentalism is not only a psychic mode of separation, it is also a psychic mode of inequality.* Within this mode the nonbeliever is profoundly unequal to the

10. These paragraphs are abridged from Stein, "Evil as Love and as Liberation," 393–420.

> believer, man is eternally unequal to God, and woman is unquestionably unequal to man. Fundamentalism is about inequality. When we think about fundamentalism, we tend to be aware of woman's inequality to man and the nonbeliever's inequality to the believer, but we tend to forget *the believer's inequality to God.* In fundamentalist regimes, God rules over men, while men rule over women. Being oppressed by God, oppressing women, fundamentalism is an *oppressed oppression.*[11]
>
> *In religious fundamentalism the figure of the father is perverted:* A father who liberates his sons (and daughters) into social life, into taking initiative, and into the joy of competence and the entitlement to pursue their desires in life, becomes the Father who liberates his sons (and daughters) from "themselves," that is, from their individuality, human compassion, and the moral impulse. Love for this father liberates his sons to humiliate, kill, and destroy "His" enemies. The persecutory father, who is an inner "gang leader" is rephrased as a loved and loving father, although this father is obviously a vengeful killer. Obviously, what subtends this love of God is tremendous, transformed hatred, a kind of *loving paranoia.*[12]

Stein's analysis reveals very clearly the pathway to comprehending the roots of fundamentalist violence. She is describing what happens when the dimensions of self (temporal) and other (horizontal) become anxiety-producing, distressing, overwhelming. In this situation, the vertical relation to God becomes the escape valve that allows one to transcend this world of materiality. She does not use the term "Gnosticism," but she is describing its spiritual core: the desire to escape to a higher world of spiritual perfection beyond the physical world we know.[13]

~

We have considered a particular form of terrorism as an example of unbalanced consciousness that is a God-centered, vertical idolatry. As

11. Stein, "Fundamentalism, Father and Son, and Vertical Desire," 209–10.

12. Ibid., 224.

13. Barry Cooper has provided another key commentary on the psychopathology of Al Qaeda in his book *The New Political Religions.* Cooper expresses well the idea that the "nostalgia" of the fundamentalist personality type is an optical illusion. The longing for the past is a mask covering up an alienation of the self from the authentic reality of the tradition.

we shift our attention now to the Self-centered personality type, we ask in what sense it leads to morally problematic situations.

There are some clear examples of pathological behavior that we can point to. A person robs a convenience store, killing the cashier. The person is desperate for money to support a drug habit. In a case such as this, selfhood has collapsed into an egocentricity that is so intense that it has no ability to be concerned for the welfare of other human beings. Rape is another example of this sort of pathological behavior.

The shooting rampage at Virginia Tech University on April 16, 2007, is an even more dramatic case. The mentally ill gunman killed thirty-two people before committing suicide. In Kierkegaard's terms, suicide can be understood as the final act of a completely collapsed self in despair. The pain of existence caused by the pressure to grow psychologically becomes unbearable; the pain is ended through suicide. In Girard's terms, the more common pattern of violence is a lynch mob attacking an individual, but in some situations the dynamic flips over and the individual attacks the "crowd" that he delusionally believes is persecuting him. The gunman's videotaped comments revealed that he saw himself as a scapegoat, dying "like Christ." This incident is a powerful illustration of Girard's concept of the satanic roots of violence. The lynch mob has a satanic structure, but in some cases the demons of violence congregate in one person and then explode into the world like a bolt of lightning.

It is easy to point to examples such as this without being made uncomfortable because the "I" who is doing the pointing is usually an average, law-abiding citizen; but we really ought to be uncomfortable. I say this because in the contemporary West the cultural atmosphere in which we live is dominated by the assumptions and myths of modern individualism, and these assumptions are problematic.[14] If human beings are atomized individuals fundamentally separated from each other, then there is no intrinsic obligation for human beings to be concerned about the welfare of others. We may share our financial resources with

14. See Cunningham, *These Three Are One*, 171: "The notion of the self as subjective consciousness displaced the centrality of mutual participation, both in the doctrine of God and in the Christian understanding of human community. The outcome is visible all around us; in its glorification of the isolated individual, our culture is profoundly antitrinitarian. At every level, through practically every system and structure, we are discouraged from allowing our lives to become too tightly intertwined with those of others."

others or spend everything on our own desires, as it suits our whim. We can spend our time helping to build houses for the disadvantaged, or waste it all playing violent video games, as it suits our whim. We can educate ourselves about the impact our consumerist lifestyle has on the environment, and change our habits accordingly, or bury our head in the sand, as it suits our whim. We can be actively engaged in thinking about and discussing with others how humanity can be transformed for the better, or we can live lives of intellectual sloth, as it suits our whim. I could go on building this list, but I will stop there, the point having been sufficiently raised. I am suggesting that the most extreme forms of pathology are canaries in the coalmine rather than unpredictable aberrations from normality. To the extent that atomized existence is considered the normal and normative way for human beings to live, the criminal is simply taking the way we live to its logical conclusion. As one of Bruce Cockburn's songs says: "the trouble with normal is it always gets worse."

If individuals commit illegal acts, we call it *crime*. But if a society functions in a manner that ignores, humiliates, or discriminates against a part of that society, then it is called *injustice*. Consider the manner in which African-Americans have been treated in the United States for hundreds of years. The issue I am raising here is that the philosophy of modern individualism is *intrinsically unjust* because it teaches people that they have no obligations whatsoever to be concerned about the welfare of other human beings. In order for society to be fundamentally just, it must be made up of persons who understand that the lives of all human beings are interconnected.[15] We are not atomized units of selfish desire, but social creatures who thrive when we live *with* and *for* others. Karl Barth expresses this idea powerfully, illustrating effectively the interconnection of the dimensions of reality:

> [Man's] ignorance of God culminates and manifests itself in his ignorance of his fellow man. He regards him as an object to whom he as subject may or may not be in relation according to his own free choice and disposal. . . . By chance or caprice or free judgment he can just as well be to him a tyrant or slave as a free supporter, just as well a hater as an admirer, a foe as

15. Linell Cady helpfully develops this line of thought in chapter 3 of *Religion, Theology, and American Public Life*. See especially 83–84, where she argues that the atomization of society lays the groundwork for totalitarianism.

> a friend, a corrupter as a helper. He can be one thing to one person and another to another, or now one thing, now another, to the same person. In relationship to his fellow man, also, he exists in total ambivalence, . . . If man knew the true and living God who himself became man in the one Jesus Christ, who in divine faithfulness gave himself to all men, and united himself with them, then only faithfulness (and not a faithfulness which is constantly accompanied and shot through with unfaithfulness) would be possible between his fellow man and himself, himself and his fellow man. Recognizing themselves in the God who is true God and true man, man and fellow man can wish to live not without or against one another, but only with one another. If they can be and, in fact, always are so divided in their relationship to one another, if man can be important to man, a neighbor, friend, and helper, and yet at any moment indifferent, a stranger, enemy, and corrupter, if he can be and actually is to him more of a wolf than a person—all this is a manifestation of the ambivalence in the relationship to God.[16]

If we think that being simply "left alone" to pursue our own individually chosen ends is the ultimate high point of human culture, then we are failing to recognize that we will reap what we sow. A society of atomized individuals is going to have all of the pathologies that ours has. In the language of the dimensions of reality, to try to live solely in the selfhood dimension, while alienating ourselves from our sociality and from nature and from God is a warped and unbalanced way of living. It is not the high point of human evolution but a side eddy that can and has turned into a destructive vortex leading either to mindless and false forms of "happiness" or to the despair seen in the drug addict and the crazed gunman. Kierkegaard's *The Sickness unto Death* is describing *us*.

~

The controversy regarding abortion is pertinent here, though I need to tread very carefully in what I say. I must either write a full book-length treatment of all of the complexities of the issue, or say next to nothing. I have chosen the latter path.

When a person such as Paul Hill murders an abortion doctor, believing that he is obeying the will of God, the vertical psychological pattern is essentially the same as that which I have described in connection

16. Barth, *Christian Life*, 131–32.

with the 9/11 hijackers. Mark Juergensmeyer's book *Terror in the Mind of God* has interviews with Christian, Jewish, and Muslim fundamentalists who have either engaged in acts of violence or have supported those who did. I recommend that work to fill out this aspect of the picture.

The Roe v. Wade decision was one of those rare moments in history when the shifting of power from one dimension of reality to another takes place, making visible what is usually unseen. In the American and French Revolutions, we could feel the balance of power shifting from the monarchic principle to the democratic principle (from the vertical to the horizontal), and in Roe v. Wade we could feel another seismic shift to the individualistic principle (the temporal trajectory of selfhood). In a certain sense, those who argue for these shifts are conscious of what they are doing; but in another sense they are not, because they do not see the bigger picture of the three dimensions of reality. They are partisans of a narrow principle, without seeing their role in the larger drama that is the human condition.

The picture of the dimensions of existence that I have been sketching in this book enables us to understand why there is such a wide variety of views in the modern world regarding what constitutes "tyranny." We can note, for example, that the arguments in favor of choice focus on the tyranny of the state in denying individual rights, or of religious people imposing their views on others, or of men seeking to control women. We can note on the other side the arguments that use phrases such as "the slaughter of the innocents" to evoke the tyranny of King Herod. The abortion debate is so intractable because people who are struggling against tyranny are by definition righteous in their own eyes. The evil is always on the other side if one is struggling for freedom and against tyranny.

If one considers American history in general, such language is always used in large-scale moral and political events. The American Revolution threw off the tyranny of the King of England. The Civil War was an argument between those who saw slavery as tyranny and those who rejected federal tyranny in favor of "states rights." The twentieth century saw wars against Axis tyranny and Communist tyranny. The twenty-first century has emerged as a war against "Islamo-fascist tyranny." Everyone is enthusiastic about labeling other people as tyrants, but it is psychically impossible to see oneself as a tyrant.[17] In the context of this book, the salient point is that when people "climb out on a limb" by emphasizing one dimension of reality to the exclusion of others, they develop a vision of what constitutes tyranny *from their perspective . . . on that limb*. The normative concept that we ought to work with is that any progress toward social healing in relation to the very painful topic of abortion is only going to come from an increasing ability to see things from multiple perspectives and to hold the dimensions in creative tension.

I invite my reader to reflect further on the arguments that swirl around the abortion debate, while keeping in mind the anthropology I have been developing in this book. He or she will likely find that to be a very thought-provoking exercise.[18]

I turn now to comments on Nazism and Marxism as examples of the horizontal personality type. In my earlier book, *The Genealogy of Violence*, I argued that the scapegoats killed by the Nazis represented the future, the possibility of spiritual transformation, and that the scapegoats killed by Stalin represented the past, the underdevelopment of humanity that was supposedly being left behind by the Revolution.[19] Living in the future means that one is distancing oneself from the divinely judged sinfulness of the past, while living in the past means that one is rejecting God's call of forgiveness and new life. I still consider my intuition along those lines to be accurate, but I can now place the analysis within the broader context of the dimensions of reality that have come into focus for me since I wrote that book.

17. I developed this paragraph's analysis of tyranny and abortion in an MA thesis I wrote at the University of Virginia, "Abortion and the Struggle Against Tyranny in American History." The gist of the thesis is available online as "Questions on Abortion and the Struggle Against Tyranny," http://www.religion-online.org/showarticle.asp?title=1777.

18. Lloyd Steffen's edited anthology, *Abortion: A Reader*, is a good place to start. Other essays that I find insightful include: Ward, "Abortion as a Sacrament: Mimetic Desire and Sacrifice in Sexual Politics"; Swope, "Abortion: A Failure to Communicate"; Neuhaus, "The Religion of the Sovereign Self"; Callahan, "Abortion and the Sexual Agenda"; Grant, *English-Speaking Justice*; Manent, *The City of Man*, chap. 6; and Hart, "God or Nothingness."

19. Bellinger, *The Genealogy of Violence*, chap. 8.

These comments by Girard reveal that the Nazi longing was for the archaic world of sacrificial religion:

> The spiritual goal of Hitler's ideology was to root out of Germany, then all of Europe, that calling that the Christian tradition places upon all of us: the concern for victims.
>
> For evident tactical reasons, Nazism at war attempted to conceal the genocide. I think that if it had won out, it would have announced it publicly in order to show that Nazism had ended the concern for victims as the supposedly irrevocable sense of our history.
>
> But to suppose, as I do, that the Nazis clearly found in the concern for victims the dominant value of our world, isn't this to overestimate their moral and spiritual insight? I believe not. They found support in the thinker who discovered the anthropological key to Christianity: its vocation of concern for victims. I refer, of course, to Friedrich Nietzsche. (ISS, 170–71)
>
> Christian truth has been making an unrelenting historical advance in our world. Paradoxically, it goes hand in hand with the apparent decline of Christianity. The more Christianity besieges our world, in the sense that it besieged Nietzsche before his collapse, the more difficult it becomes to escape it by means of innocuous painkillers and tranquilizers such as the "humanistic" compromises of our dear old positivist predecessors. To elude his own discovery and to defend mythological violence, Nietzsche is obliged to justify *human sacrifice*, and he doesn't hesitate to do so, resorting to horrifying arguments. He raises the stakes even on the worst social Darwinism. He suggests that to avoid degenerating, societies must get rid of humans who are waste, who hinder and weigh them down:
>
>> Through Christianity, the individual was made so important, so absolute, that he could no longer *be sacrificed*: but the species endures only through human sacrifice. . . . Genuine charity demands sacrifice for the good of the species—it is hard, it is full of self-overcoming, because it *needs human sacrifice*. And this pseudo-humaneness called Christianity wants it established that *no one should be sacrificed*.[20]
>
> Weak and ill as he was, Nietzsche never misses an occasion to flagellate our modern concern for the weak and the ill. . . .

20. Girard is citing Nietzsche, *Will to Power*, 142.

> To bury the modern concern for victims under millions and millions of corpses—there you have the National Socialist way of being Nietzschean. . . . Nietzsche is the author of the only texts capable of clarifying the Nazi horror. If there is a spiritual essence of the movement, Nietzsche is the one who expresses it. (ISS, 174–75)

The fact that our universities today have Nietzscheans of various stripes on their faculties shows how difficult it is to truly learn the lessons that ought to be learned from history.

An article by Richard Koenigsberg adds an important facet to these comments by Girard on Nazism.[21] Koenigsberg argues that Hitler did not simply want to sacrifice the Jews; he also wanted to sacrifice his own soldiers. He wanted war to be a vast altar on which human sacrifices would be made to the glory of the German nation. The killing of the Jews, Koenigsberg argues, was actually a secondary, derivative goal that followed the logic of Hitler's desire to sacrifice the flower of Germany's youth. Since the idol worshipped by Hitler was the (horizontal) state, it was unthinkable that anyone would be exempt from the sacrificial unanimity. Hitler thus portrayed the Jews as egocentric individualists who would try to escape from the duty to serve the state above all other loyalties. They must not be allowed to do this; they must be forced to participate in the state as unwilling symbols of the sacrifices being made willingly by those who obeyed Hitler's orders. In Hitler's words:

> *Volksgemeinschaft* [peoples' community], overcoming bourgeois privatism, means unconditionally equating the individual fate and the fate of the nation. No one is excepted from the crisis of the Reich. This Volk is but yourselves. There may not be a single person who excludes himself from this joint obligation.[22]

Hitler was saying to the German nation that all citizens must be willing to die for the nation; if you are not, you will be killed.

~

We shift now to a consideration of Karl Marx as an example of a future-oriented utopian (horizontal) personality type. The central paradox of

21. Koenigsberg, "Sacrificial Meaning of the Holocaust," http://home.earthlink.net/~libraryofsocialscience/sacrificial_meaning.htm

22. This passage is quoted, without reference, in Koenigsberg's article, "Sacrificial Meaning of the Holocaust."

Marxism is obviously the contradiction between the professed ethical vision of social progress and the unethical means that are used to accomplish that "progress." These are brief selections from *The Communist Manifesto*.

> The bourgeoisie, wherever it has got the upper hand, has put an end to all feudal, patriarchal, idyllic relations. It has pitilessly torn asunder the motley feudal ties that bound man to his "natural superiors," and has left remaining no other nexus between man and man than naked self-interest, than callous "cash payment." It has drowned the most heavenly ecstasies of religious fervor, of chivalrous enthusiasm, of philistine sentimentalism, in the icy water of egotistical calculation. It has resolved personal worth into exchange value, and in place of the numberless indefeasible chartered freedoms, has set up that single, unconscionable freedom—Free Trade. In one word, for exploitation, veiled by religious and political illusions, it has substituted naked, shameless, direct, brutal exploitation. . . .
>
> From the moment when labor can no longer be converted into capital, money, or rent, into a social power capable of being monopolized, i.e., from the moment when individual property can no longer be transformed into bourgeois property, into capital, from that moment, you say, individuality vanishes.
>
> You must, therefore, confess that by "individual" you mean no other person than the bourgeois, than the middle-class owner of property. This person must, indeed, be swept out of the way, and made impossible. . . .
>
> The charges against Communism made from a religious, a philosophical and, generally, from an ideological standpoint, are not deserving of serious examination. . . .
>
> In place of the old bourgeois society, with its classes and class antagonisms, we shall have an association, in which the free development of each is the condition for the free development of all. . . .
>
> The Communists disdain to conceal their views and aims. They openly declare that their ends can be attained only by the forcible overthrow of all existing social conditions. Let the ruling classes tremble at a Communistic revolution. The proletarians have nothing to lose but their chains. They have a world to win. Working men of all countries, unite![23]

23. Abridged from Marx and Engels, *Marx-Engels Reader*, 473–500.

The characteristic themes of Marx's thought are clearly displayed here. There is a great historical erudition combined with a profound moral illiteracy. There is a reductionistic mentality run rampant that insists on oversimplifying the complexity of life. There is a great faith in the state as a channel of redemption. There is a war on the vertical dimension as represented by religion, and on the selfhood—individuality dimension. Everything is reduced to the horizontal dimension through a massive leveling of humanity. There is an unacknowledged belief in magic; the oppressed masses will be magically transformed into human perfection in a historical blink of an eye. The source of this magic remains a mystery; it can only be described as the "inevitable" process of history. Marx assumes that he can see this future perfection clearly as if through a crystal ball. To describe as a "tragedy" the discrepancy between Marx's vision of universal salvation and the killing fields to which his ideas led in the twentieth century is a rather large understatement.[24]

Marx's ideas were put into practice by Vladimir Lenin, as we can see in this quotation:

> Thousands of practical forms and methods of accounting and controlling the rich, the rogues and the idlers should be devised and put to a practical test by the communes themselves, by small units in town and country. Variety is a guarantee of vitality here, a pledge of success in achieving the single common aim—to cleanse the land of Russia of all sorts of harmful insects, of crook-fleas, of bedbugs—the rich, and so on and so forth. In one place half a score of rich, a dozen crooks, half a dozen workers who shirk their work . . . will be put in prison. In another place they will be put to cleaning latrines. In a third place they will be provided with "yellow tickets" after they have served their time, so that all the people shall have them under surveillance, as *harmful* persons, until they reform. In a fourth place, one out of every ten idlers will be shot on the spot. In a fifth place mixed methods may be adopted, and by probational release, for example, the rich, the bourgeois intellectuals, the crooks and hooligans who are corrigible will be given an opportunity to reform quickly. The more variety there will be, the better and richer will

24. Susan Neiman describes Marx's thought as an attempt to address the problem of evil; however, ". . . it's often noted that though Marx's tone conveys constant moral indignation, he has no moral philosophy in any standard sense—no definitions of right or justice, no attempts to establish moral foundations in general or to argue for the rightness of any action in particular." *Evil in Modern Thought*, 103.

> be our general experience, the more certain and more rapid will be the success of socialism, and the easier will it be for practice to devise—for only practice can devise—the *best* methods and means of struggle.[25]

Eric Voegelin had very personal reasons to see Marxism as one of the chief modern examples of homicidal Gnosticism. Voegelin recounts in his *Autobiographical Reflections* that a Marxist student in the 1930s regretfully informed him that "when we come to power, we have to kill you."[26] I present a small portion of Voegelin's extensive critique of Marx:

> Philosophy springs from the love of being; it is man's loving endeavor to perceive the order of being and attune himself to it. Gnosis desires dominion over being; in order to seize control of being the Gnostic constructs his system. The building of systems is a gnostic form of reasoning, not a philosophical one. (CWEV, 5:273)

> The aim of parousiastic [apocalyptic] Gnosticism is to destroy the order of being, which is experienced as defective and unjust, and through man's creative power to replace it with a perfect and just order. Now, however the order of being may be understood—as a world dominated by cosmic-divine powers in the civilizations of the Near and Far East, or as the creation of a world-transcendent God in Judaeo-Christian symbolism, or as an essential order of being in philosophical contemplation—it remains something that is given, that is not under man's control. In order, therefore, that the attempt to create a new world may seem to make sense, the givenness of the order of being must be obliterated; the order of being must be interpreted, rather, as essentially under man's control. And taking control of being further requires that the transcendent origin of being be obliterated: It requires the decapitation of being—the murder of God.
>
> The murder of God is committed speculatively by explaining divine being as the work of man.... It does not suffice, therefore, to replace the old world of God with a new world of man: the world of God itself must have been a world of man, and God a work of man that can therefore be destroyed if it prevents man from reigning over the order of being. The murder of God

25. Lenin, *Lenin Anthology*, 431–32.

26. See Heilke, *Eric Voegelin*, 184, quoting *Autobiographical Reflections* (CWEV, 34:111).

> must be made retroactive speculatively. This is the reason man's "being-of-himself" is the principal point of Marx's Gnosis. And he gets his speculative support from the explanation of nature and history as a process in which man creates himself to his full stature. The murder of God, then, is of the very essence of the gnostic re-creation of the order of being. (CWEV, 5:278–79)
>
> The nature of a thing cannot be changed; whoever tries to "alter" its nature destroys the thing. Man cannot transform himself into superman; the attempt to create a superman is an attempt to murder man. Historically, the murder of God is not followed by the superman, but by the murder of man: the deicide of the gnostic theoreticians is followed by the homicide of the revolutionary practitioners. (CWEV, 5:284)

Voegelin has penetrated to the depths of Marx's pathology as a thinker and exposed his corruption as a refusal to live in the complexity of reality, motivated by rebellion against God, with murderous results.

In summary, we can ask: How does the utopian self inhabit time? It is clear that the past is backwardness and oppression that needs to be killed off and forgotten. The future is a bright shining beacon to which we are drawn. But the present needs to be turned into a killing field in order to reach the promised land. The end justifies the means. What we normally think of as an ethical rule, such as "you shall not kill," can be suspended if we convince ourselves that we will only reach a state of ethical perfection by rejecting ethics. The new command that we give ourselves, since we have installed ourselves in the place of God, is: "*we shall kill* in order to make the world *a better place*."

~

We are now in a position to formulate a thesis of Christian political science: When human beings fail to live in expansive relation to the triune God, their personalities will become narrowed down in an orientation toward one dimension of reality, and they will enter into conflict with other human beings whose personalities are also narrowed, either in a different orientation, or, in the same orientation but in a different subculture (i.e., Christian vs. Muslim fundamentalists).

Forms of Unbalanced Consciousness Become Violent Because They Are Seeking to Overcome Evil with Evil

The principle that ties these personality types (fundamentalism, individualism, utopianism) together is *overcoming evil with evil.* Human beings as moral agents identify something wrong with the world, some "evil" or negative situation that needs to be changed or overcome. The means that are commonly used to bring about this change are themselves morally problematic, however. (1) Islam began as a movement against idolatry, yet there are Muslims today who have turned God into an idol who commands them to overcome the "Great Satan" United States by killing civilians with airplanes. Jewish and Christian fundamentalists have also committed acts of violence on the world stage, expressing their rage and frustration at modernity. (2) Modern individualism and autonomy is supposedly the fruit of the Enlightenment's emancipation of the human spirit from the bondage of religious superstition; yet when this emancipation leads to a society in which evil is understood as *anything that restricts ME*, the flipside of our pursuit of selfish goods is a callous disregard for the welfare and flourishing of other human lives. (3) Marxism presented itself to the world as a form of salvation; the formula that would allow human beings to save themselves from the negative effects of their own greed had supposedly been found. Yet this "salvation" cure turned out to be much worse than the disease. In Karl Barth's words: "Far more than the conservative, the revolutionary is *overcome of evil*, because with his 'No' he stands so strangely near to God. This is the tragedy of revolution. Evil is not the true answer to evil."[27]

Jesus was accused of casting out demons by the power of the ruler of demons. He responded: "How can Satan cast out Satan? If a kingdom is divided against itself, that kingdom will not be able to stand" (Mark 3:23–24). In the wake of Girard's thought, this passage is clarified greatly. Satan is both the one who sows disorder, chaos, rivalry, conflict, and he is also the one who ends the chaos and restores a peaceful sense of "law and order" through the scapegoat mechanism.[28] (Good) violence casts out (bad) violence, as the plot of numberless television shows and movies reminds us. These two aspects of Satan inhabit two of the three

27. Barth, *Epistle to the Romans*, 480.

28. See the chapter on "Satan" in *The Girard Reader*, and also Mark Heim's useful survey of this topic in *Saved from Sacrifice*, 147–53.

dimensions we have been analyzing. Mimetic desire leading to chaos happens on the horizontal plane; the sacrifice that restores order is the blade of the guillotine that comes down from above; it is the transcendent, sacred solution to the crisis. Satan also has a third face relating to the individual vector; here he is the voice of the Tempter speaking to the individual. The Tempter sows the discontent, suspicion, and discord that later flower into mimetic desire on the social plane.

Three Faces of Satan

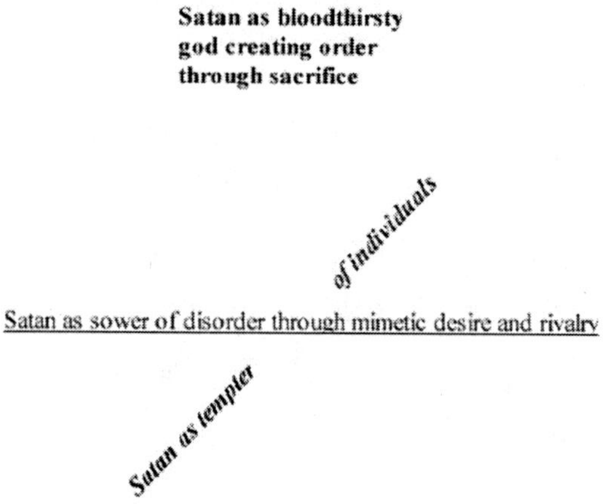

When human beings seek to overcome evil with evil, they are following the script written by Satan. The deepest ethical challenge that faces us is learning how to overcome evil *with good*. I will have more to say on this topic at a later point in the text, in the context of my discussion of war and pacifism.

Different Ways of Thinking and Living Arise out of Deep Choices

In the preceding theses, I developed a *phenomenology* of three basic approaches to interpreting reality (fundamentalism, individualism, utopianism). I described these patterns of thought and life as anthropological phenomena that have identifiable general features and characteristics, as they inhabit the dimensions of reality in distorted ways. But this is not yet a *genealogy*, which is the next important step to take in the enquiry. When we notice the differences between the personality types, and their similarities, we still have not worked our way down to an understanding of these phenomena at a deeper level. We need to ask where these approaches come from. How does a human being become a fundamentalist? How does a human being become an individualist? How does a human being become a utopian? I express the questions in this repetitive manner to emphasize that we start out in the center; we come from the hand of God as human beings made in God's image. We then move away from that center and climb out on our preferred limb, our overemphasized dimension.

This brings us to a topic that is difficult to grasp clearly: we are making choices, but we are not necessarily making these choices *consciously*. How can one make choices unconsciously? This is the paradox. I have no easy answers here. I am simply noting the problem.[29] To reflect on this paradox we need to consider the concepts of time and freedom.

What is time? At the deepest level, time is the procession of the creative speech of God. In other words, there is time because God does not create everything in an instant. God is not like a magician who says "Poof!" and the entire universe in its finished form is there. Rather, God creates slowly, patiently, as an extended event. Creation is the going forth, the procession, of God's speech. God is *roomy*, allowing space for the existence of beings outside of God. As Robert Jenson puts it: "God as Father, Son, and Spirit can make room in himself for others, and the room that he makes is our created time. The opening of that room is the act of creation."[30]

Human beings are one of God's creatures. We are different from the other creatures in that we have the potential to be aware of the event of creation and our place in it. In the terms of our analysis here, our uniqueness lies in our ability to comprehend that we inhabit the dimensions of reality: the vertical, the temporal, and the horizontal. We live as natural beings in relation to God, as selves in time, and as social beings.

29. Readers who are familiar with Kierkegaard's *Sickness unto Death* will recognize that he was attempting to gain a better understanding of this.

30. Jenson, *Systematic Theology: Volume I*, 226.

We can nuance this perspective by noticing that time is not just one thing, but a phenomenon that inhabits the dimensions in a complex way. The vertical axis of God and nature is itself a timeline. The story told by natural science goes like this: first there was the Big Bang, fourteen billion years ago; the galaxies, stars, and planets were formed over billions of years; on earth, life appeared; life developed into increasingly complex forms with eyesight, consciousness, etc., over many millions of years; human beings appeared and eventually gained the ability to understand the history that led up to them. We can refer to this timeline as *cosmic time*, the history of the universe that preceded human beings.

In this book I have been stressing the selfhood dimension as a trajectory of time in which human beings exist in between the past and the future. This is *psychological time* and *historical consciousness*.

The horizontal plane also has a temporal dimension, though it is not as easy to see as the other two. This quotation from Girard points us in the right direction:

> From a Christian standpoint, ancient theories of the Eternal Return contain some truth since they know about these cycles [chaos—sacrifice—order] which are the same thing as the "self-organizing system" of Satan, but they cannot discover the engine that powers the cycles, the foundational power of the mimetic consensus, or victimage mechanism, or generative scapegoating.
>
> The end of this circular time, the shift from an eternally recurring world to a time which has a real beginning and a real end is inseparable from the revelation of the force that until the Judaic and Christian revelation had powered the cycles but now loses its effectiveness as a result of being revealed.
>
> We must envisage this shift from a circular to a linear temporality in conjunction with the idea that the Cross is a decisive defeat for Satan, the end of his kingdom, which follows logically from the whole mimetic interpretation. (TGR, 205)

Human culture has an archaic form that is constituted by scapegoating. This form construes time as cyclical; the sacrifices must be repeated over and over again. It is hard to imagine a clearer example of this than the pre-Columbian practice of human sacrifice in Central America, which ensured that the Sun would rise each day. The writer of the book of Hebrews had something similar in mind when he spoke of the temple sacrifices that had to be continually repeated; Christ was, in contrast, the sacrifice to end all sacrifices. The biblical revelation makes possible an exodus of humanity from sacrifice by opening up time as a trajectory of growth toward God's peaceableness. The horizontal plane is thus characterized by a *cultural time* that has a cyclical (violent) earlier form and a progressive (nonviolent) later form. The other two forms of time, cosmic and psychological, are both progressive views that tell a past—present—future story; these two forms of historical awareness were in fact made possible by the impact of divine revelation on the horizontal plane's circular time. This passage from Stanley Hauerwas is one of his brain-rattling pithy comments: "Without the church the world would have no history. Such a claim is not just a 'confessional' stance but the most determinative realist claim Christians can possibly make."[31]

This idea, that cosmic and psychological time were made possible by biblical revelation, can be seen in the observation that Western science developed out of biblical roots, and that the "individual" or the "person" is a product of biblical faith. The second idea, concerning the individual, is one of Kierkegaard's main concerns, as we have seen; a similar perspective is articulated by John Zizioulas: "The person, both as a concept and as a living reality, is purely the product of patristic thought."[32] Glenn Tinder has also spoken of the "exalted individual" as a Western idea that has biblical roots.[33] Against the backdrop of these interpretations, it becomes clear that our awareness of the dimensions of reality has been unpacked or "differentiated" (in Voegelin's term) by biblical revelation. The primordial default setting of human consciousness, which is scapegoating and cyclical time, can now be clearly seen as a refusal to live in that *real* time that is God's work of complexifying creation. Human sin, at its most basic root, generates a fake second reality and a false circular time by rejecting divine time, which is a trajectory, a movement toward God's kingdom.

~

The picture of time that has just been painted has a crucial corollary: freedom. Freedom is the central gift from God that sets human beings apart from the other animals. We tend to think of freedom in somewhat superficial terms as the ability to make choices. But at a deeper level our

31. Hauerwas, *Christian Existence Today*, 61.

32. Zizioulas, *Being as Communion*, 27.

33. See Tinder, "Can We Be Good Without God?"

freedom is seen in the possibility that our souls can be oriented toward what is good for us and for others, or they can be oriented toward what is harmful. How these orientations come about through our "choice" is one of the deepest mysteries of life. I have no easy answer that can explain this mystery. I can, however, affirm the view that when our freedom is understood rightly as an orientation toward the good, it is not something that we *have*, it is something that we *participate in*. Freedom is a phenomenon of community.[34] What we superficially call "freedom," as the ability to make choices on our own, should more appropriately be called license.

Human beings face genuine forks in the road of existence that are not faced by the lower animals. Usually (and paradoxically), we choose to take these forks at a very deep level of our emotions, a level that lies below our everyday self-conscious awareness and choice-making ability. Imagine that there are four people walking down a pathway that represents this choice-making activity. We will name these people 1A, 1B, 2A, and 2B. The four persons come to a fork in the road, at which they must choose what their attitude will be toward the divinely directed ongoing event of creation. Two persons (2A and 2B) choose to have an accepting attitude, and two (1A and 1B) turn the other way, rejecting the uncertainty of ongoing creation in favor of a more static form of existence that they think they can control. These two walk further, coming to another fork, at which they must choose again. The first, 1A, chooses a path that represents a socially pre-established form of existence that the individual passively conforms to. The other, 1B, chooses a path that requires the individual to be very self-assertive and focused on his or her own needs and desires, in defiance of society and God. The two people who made the initial choice to have an accepting attitude toward the event of ongoing creation have also continued walking. They come to the next fork in the road. 2A chooses to seize the initiative and take control of the event of creation, forcing it to conform to their vision of how things ought to be in the future. 2B takes the pathway that represents a recognition that God is the creator of the universe, not human beings. This traveler adopts a humble attitude, seeking to follow the guidance and instruction that comes from above, so that he or she will be able find their place in the world, cooperating constructively with

34. See Jenson, *On Thinking the Human*, chap. 3.

God's ongoing work. These forks in the road and the main possibilities that they map out lead to the psychological types that we observe in our modern world. This chart will hopefully clarify the preceding sentences, which may have been a little hard to follow:

	the ongoing event of creation			
	↙ rejection		↘ acceptance	
	↙	↘	↙	↘
	1A	1B	2A	2B
emotional posture	passivity	Self-assertiveness	arrogance	humility
psycho-logical type	fundamentalist	individualist	utopian	maturing person
temporal center of gravity	past	Present	future	the fullness of time

What are the choices that human beings are making very deep in their souls that lead to them becoming fundamentalists, or individualists, or utopian revolutionaries? It is not simply a matter of being persuaded by certain arguments. There is a deeper emotional level at work that is difficult to unearth archaeologically. This chart is just scratching the surface of a topic that is very difficult to visualize.

A basic distinction is traditionally made between the realm of eternity and transcendence (which is unchanging), and the realm of materiality (which is changing and perishing). In these terms, a fundamentalist is one who rejects life within materiality and seeks to live a fully transcendent life. The fundamentalist's rigidity of thought and rejection of ongoing creation in this world is an attempt to fly away prematurely to the unchangeableness of heaven. The individualist seems to take the opposite path of embracing materiality and change. But this is a shallow and illusory choice because the individualist wants everything to change except him or herself; he or she is also rejecting ongoing creation, along with the fundamentalist.[35] The utopian is apparently

35. On the irony of modern "liberals" wanting everything to change except them-

accepting the concept of transformation of this world according to an ideal of perfection, but he or she is arrogantly playing the role of God. The utopian wants to be the change agent without having been changed by God first. This leads directly into the abyss that Eric Voegelin describes as trying to "immanentize the eschaton," trying to bring heaven to earth through human efforts alone.

Philosopher Charles Taylor has written a book on *The Sources of the Self*. With no disrespect intended toward his magisterial work, what I am suggesting flips the singular and the plural: "the Source and the selves." We can understand various forms of modern selfhood as deflections from relationship with the triune God; these anthropological phenomena are partial theological truths that turn into falsehoods precisely because they are partial and narrow rather than expansive and complex. Fundamentalism is correct to focus on the scriptures as the vital channel of divine revelation to humanity, but its interpretation of the scriptures is derailed by the psychological immaturity of the interpreters. The dignity of the individual, which is affirmed in the modern West, is a historical fruit of the Christian message, but this gift has been turned into the arrogant usurpation of the place of God by the isolated and autonomous Self. It is a commonplace to see Marxism as a transmuted form of the prophetic (social and political) strand of the Judeo-Christian tradition. To the extent that people of faith have had no real vision for the future, they made possible the human attempt to shape a future without God.[36] The pathologies of the modern world are to a great extent the result of the Christian tradition's failure to present a truthful understanding of God's character and purposes in the world, and its failure to articulate and live out a healthy anthropology—an anthropology of authentic freedom in communion with God and the neighbor.[37]

---

selves, see Reno, *In the Ruins of the Church*, 98.

36. See Moltmann, "Hope and History," 369–70.

37. See David Cayley's summary of Ivan Illich: "What is original with Illich is the idea that the modern West, as defined by its characteristic attempt to manipulate others for their own salvation, is a *perversion* of Christian faith." Illich, *The Rivers North of the Future*, 29. A key theme in the book is "the corruption of the best is the worst"; in other words, the perversion of Christianity produces dire effects.

(The fourth personality type, 2B, signifies the ideal of human development. I will amplify that vision later in this book, particularly in the comments on faith, hope, and love in a later section of Part Two.)

The Deepest Root of Violence is the Self's Refusal to Grow Spiritually

The profound question regarding why human beings are violent can be answered along the following lines. *Truth* is accumulative; our consciousness will be shaped by truth to the extent that we allow ourselves to be educated by the wisdom that comes from God and has been mediated to us through our philosophical and religious traditions. *The Good* is the fruit of maturation; human beings become ethical as they allow themselves to be drawn upward so that they participate in God's love for humanity. The ability to perceive the *Beauty* of the world and to live a beautiful life is a gift from God. Violence rejects this journey of growth into the fullness of what it means to be a human being; it prefers a stunted life that produces falsehood, evil, and ugliness. We can specify precisely the deepest root of pathological violence as the resistance of the human being to the growth, expansion, and increasing complexity that are the marks of living into the image of God in which we are created.

Why do we resist growth? We human beings are distinct from the lower animals in our ability to experience angst, which is an emotion arising from our ambivalence about our existence in time. Angst, or anxiety, results from desiring and fearing the same thing at the same time, which is the possibility of our spiritual development. Kierkegaard describes this as "a sympathetic antipathy and an antipathetic sympathy" (CA, 42). We have been created, but we are still coming into existence; the event of creation is still happening within us, which fills us with anxiety. We invent strategies that seek to manage this anxiety and keep it in check. To the extent that we are narcissistic we seek comfort and avoid pain. To be open to growth toward maturity involves a willingness to endure the pain of dying to oneself and being reborn. If we are unwilling to go through this pain, the result will be our attempts to make others feel pain in the false belief that by doing so we will avoid it.

Fundamentalism, individualistic aestheticism, and utopianism are all examples of human inventiveness when it comes to evading the call of creation. They are forms of immature selfhood that seek to fend off the possibility of mature selfhood. If we dimly perceive the possibility that our self could die and be replaced by another self, we must prevent this by construing the more mature self as an *other*, an *alien*, rather than as the true self that we are called to be. This is the root of the rejection of *otherness* that our modern culture notices but can only respond to with calls for "tolerance." We attack the Other because *we do not want to become an other to ourselves* through the event of spiritual death and rebirth. *We become violent when we try to maintain the current shape of our immature, unbalanced, and contracted consciousness (against the possibility that it could become mature, balanced, and expansive) by attacking the alien Other that has been generated out of our fear of growth.* In other words, violence against others begins with the invisible spiritual act of doing violence to the potential development of one's own selfhood.[38] This is the foundational, shared spiritual condition of the fundamentalists, the individualists, and the revolutionaries. We usually do not notice this underlying commonality because we are bedazzled by the surface disparities between them.[39]

I have provided an overview of how the dimensions help us to understand the roots of violence. The following theses shift to an exposition of the theological foundations that have made this anthropological analysis possible.

The Earth Has Never Been Flat

Imagine someone saying:

In the Middle Ages people believed that the world was flat. Then Copernicus came along and through his scientific investigations he came to realize that the earth is round and that it revolves around the sun once a year. Other scientists such as Kepler and Galileo confirmed and

38. See Bellinger, *The Genealogy of Violence*, 67. Michael Ignatieff makes a similar point: "Violence must be done to the self before it can be done to others. Living tissue of connection and recognition must be cauterized before a neighbor is reinvented as an enemy." *The Warrior's Honor*, 54. See also José Ortega y Gasset, who argues along similar lines in chapter 8 of *The Revolt of the Masses*.

39. Mark Juergensmeyer makes a related observation when he points out the underlying similarities of vision in Muslims, Christians, and Jews who have carried out violent attacks in recent years. See *Terror in the Mind of God*, 59.

developed Copernicus' insights. Since then, modern science has been on a progressive forward march, and religious superstition has been retreating into the shadows. One day in the future, all people will be fully intelligent, which means that they will be fully secular, with no religious beliefs what soever. The human race will then be perfectly peaceful because we modern scientists know that religion is the prime cause of violence.[40]

What's wrong with this picture? I will start with the first sentence. In fact, people in the Middle Ages knew the world was round. The ancient Greeks, such as Plato and Aristotle, et al., understood that the earth was a sphere. This knowledge was not lost in the Middle Ages; it was continued by Augustine, Bede, Aquinas, Dante, and so forth, on up to the time of Copernicus. Copernicus was not establishing that the earth was round. That was common knowledge among all the intellectuals of his day. According to historian Edward Grant, there were no educated people in the fifteenth century in Europe who would have denied that the earth is a sphere.[41] Copernicus' breakthrough was to understand that the spherical earth is not the center of the universe, around which everything else revolves. Rather, the earth rotates around its own axis once a day and revolves around the sun once a year. The arguments before his time did not concern the flat earth but rather how large the sphere of the earth is and whether or not there is land on the other side of the earth, and whether or not that land could possibly be inhabited by human beings who were not descended from Adam and Eve. When Columbus proposed sailing westward to Asia, resistance to the idea was not based on a fear of falling off the edge of the flat earth, but rather on a fear that the distance around the globe to Asia was too far. It was feared that he and his crew would die of thirst and hunger because they could not stock enough provisions to survive such a long journey. At that time, the existence of North and South America was not known to Europeans, so they believed that there was just one giant body of water consisting of what we now call the Atlantic and Pacific oceans.

What I have just been explaining may come as a surprise to you. You may have been under the impression until just now that people in the Middle Ages believed that the earth was flat. I thought that for many

40. My sarcastic tone here reflects the main argument of Jacques Ellul's *The New Demons*, which is that the modern world is just as religious as previous ages. Our idols have changed, but our superstition has not.

41. Grant, *Physical Science in the Middle Ages*, 61.

years, and I am a fairly well-educated person. I gave talks to various audiences, which included many professors, in which I said that "people in the Middle Ages believed the earth was flat." I was never corrected in this error until I gave a talk at Cornell University and Professor Carol Delaney of Stanford University, who was in the audience, mentioned the error in my historical understanding. I am saying this because my own experience has proven how widespread the urban legend about medieval belief in a flat earth actually is. It is a legend that is accepted without question by almost everyone in the Western world regardless of their educational level. The people who are most likely to recognize the fallacy in this legend are a small handful of medievalist historians, and their efforts to correct the error have obviously not been successful.

But where did this urban legend come from? Jeffrey Burton Russell has written a small book called *Inventing the Flat Earth* that answers this question.[42] It turns out that the assertion that "people in the Middle Ages believed the earth was flat" was fabricated by certain nineteenth-century authors, such as Washington Irving, Antoine-Jean Letronne, and John Draper, who had an axe to grind against religion. They saw the Enlightenment as the pathway of escape from the ignorance and superstition of theological belief systems. Therefore they produced historically biased accounts of Columbus, Copernicus, and Galileo, portraying them as the great liberators of the human mind from the darkness of religious dogmatism. Their mythical medieval opponents were portrayed as mental midgets who insisted upon believing that the earth was flat because they were committed to "biblical literalism" and opposed to the process of "scientific discovery."

In other words, these authors who concocted the "flat earth" legend were perfect exemplars of the human tendency to reject the "truth is accumulative" model of knowing in favor of a model that sees the past as darkness that must be rejected in contrast with a glorious modernity that must be accepted. The fact that this legend caught on and spread throughout Western culture shows that almost everyone in modern Western culture has a negatively biased attitude toward the Middle Ages. The legend met a felt psychological need to distance oneself from the past so that it would have no claim on shaping one's development as a human being.

42. Russell, *Inventing the Flat Earth: Columbus and Modern Historians.*

This puts the concept of a "New Copernican Revolution" in an interesting light. We need to gain an improved understanding of the psychology of violence, which will be analogous to an improved understanding of the physical universe. But the main obstacle to this new understanding of violence is not faith and theology; on the contrary, it is rejection of theology that is the obstacle. The biased modern view that sees the past as worthless cuts off the possibility of learning from the philosophical and theological traditions of Western culture, and it is these traditions that give us the key insights into human behavior that we need. The truth of this statement has been fleshed out in the writings of Kierkegaard, Voegelin, and Girard, who draw the substance of their arguments from Plato, Aristotle, the Bible, Augustine, Aquinas, and so forth. Copernicus was struggling against a worldview that insisted that the whole universe revolved around the earth, in other words, around the human observer. He broke open this narrow human-centered way of knowing and allowed for a fuller appreciation of the immense scope of creation. Modernist thinkers today who insist that we have nothing to learn from the past and that we must manufacture truth out of own heads are thus the analogs of Copernicus' opponents, not of Copernicus.[43]

If we insist that there is no divine source of truth with which human beings ought to become attuned, we will not make progress in understanding ourselves. In order to truly comprehend ourselves we need to realize that we are not the center of the universe, God is. But the massive trend of most modern and postmodern philosophy moves in precisely the opposite direction. Therefore our modern "knowledge" is actually a form of ignorance. To counter this ignorance, our minds need to be opened up to an understanding of psychological derailment, on

43. David Hart argues similarly: "Kant's 'Copernican revolution' might better be called 'Ptolemaic': if Copernicus overthrew the commonsense geocentrism of ancient cosmology by advancing the heliocentric thesis, displacing the center from "here" to "there," Kant enacted at the transcendental level an entirely contrary motion . . . Now the phenomena would revolve around the unyielding earth of apperception; again, we would stand at the center." *The Beauty of the Infinite*, 137. See also a similar argument by Olivier Clément in *On Human Being*, 10: ". . . *metanoia* [is] *the turning round* of our self-awareness, the Copernican shift of the self (individual or collective) from geocentric to heliocentric, enabling us to see in the depth of everything around us the furnace of the divine sun."

the one hand, and psychological health, on the other, that is the fruit of theological insights into the human condition.

Proper Method Consists of (1) Theology, (2) Psychology, and (3) Ethics

Significant philosophical insights in the truth-is-accumulative mode have been articulated by Alasdair MacIntyre. He has argued forcefully that we need to appreciate the wisdom of the Middle Ages and the ancient world. He presents the thought of Thomas Aquinas (1224–1274) as a model for understanding personhood and rationality. Thomas' vision in his *Summa Theologiae* is comprehensive, beginning with *theology* in the "Prima Pars" (an understanding of God and creation), moving through *psychology* in the "Prima Secundae Partis" (an understanding of how the human intellect and emotions work), leading then to *ethics* in the "Secunda Secundae Partis" (an understanding of how virtues shape the human soul and guide our actions and relations to others in appropriate ways). This is another refraction of the vertical / selfhood / horizontal pattern. This vision was made possible by Thomas' synthesis of the biblical and Greek philosophical traditions. In the modern world, the ability to perceive reality at this level of comprehensiveness has to a large extent been lost. When "modern" people have a biased attitude toward the past, rejecting the possibility of being nurtured by its wisdom, then our culture breaks apart into subcultures that cling to distorted fragments of the past that cannot be put together into a coherent whole. These subcultures shrilly attack one another with superficial slogans. In other words, MacIntyre is arguing that the only pathway that leads into a constructive form of rational debate in the future is a pathway that arises out of a respectful appropriation of the past.[44] His comments on higher education are instructive:

> Suppose it were the case that the catastrophe of which my hypothesis speaks [the Enlightenment] had occurred before, or largely before, the founding of academic history, so that the moral and other evaluative presuppositions of academic history derived from the forms of the disorder which it brought about. Suppose, that is, that the standpoint of academic history is such

44 MacIntyre, *After Virtue: A Study in Moral Theory* and *Three Rival Versions of Moral Enquiry: Encyclopaedia, Genealogy, and Tradition.*

> that from its value-neutral viewpoint moral disorder must remain largely invisible. All that the historian—and what is true of the historian is characteristically true also of the social scientist—will be allowed to perceive by the canons and categories of his discipline will be one morality succeeding another: seventeenth-century Puritanism, eighteenth-century hedonism, the Victorian work-ethic and so on, but the very language of order and disorder will not be available to him. If this were to be so, it would at least explain why what I take to be the real world and its fate has remained unrecognized by the academic curriculum. For the forms of the academic curriculum would turn out to be among the symptoms of the disaster whose occurrence the curriculum does not acknowledge.[45]

In other words, our grasp of reality is so poor as moderns because we have rejected the truth-is-accumulative method of Aquinas in favor of the truth-is-whatever-I-assert-it-is method. Our educational system is set up not simply to favor the latter method, but more crucially to keep the truth-is-accumulative method invisible to us.

The basic questions we should be asking are these: Who is God? Who are we? What should we do and say? *An understanding of who God is as Creator forms the basis of a sound psychological self-understanding, both of which are necessary as the foundation for ethical reflection.*[46] A contrast can obviously be drawn between this method and the disordered forms of life that are so prominent in the modern world. When human life becomes derailed, a corrupted *psychology* leads to an idolatrous *theology* (or to rejection of theology) and to *unethical actions*. The right ordering of method becomes scrambled. In other words, method is not just an "idea"; it is a form of life. It is what Eric Voegelin calls the order or disorder of the human soul.

Ethics has very clearly stated for millenia that murder is wrong: "Thou shalt not kill." This is a basic teaching of all major religions and philosophies. So, if we say about situations such as the Holocaust and

45. Ibid., 4.

46. This is my one sentence summary of Kierkegaard's thought. His pseudonym Vigilius Haufniensis is very concerned with the relationships between dogmatics, psychology, and ethics in *The Concept of Anxiety*. For example: "The science that deals with the explanation [of the origin of sin] is psychology, but it can explain only up to the explanation and above all must guard against leaving the impression of explaining that which no science can explain and that which ethics explains further only by presupposing it by way of dogmatics" (CA, 39).

Rwanda that these are examples of a rule being broken, then what do we say next? Ethics needs to be about more than just saying to people that what they are doing is wrong. Ethics needs to be about thinking seriously and creatively about how the human race can change and move in the direction of ethical maturity.

The problem with the common philosophical approach to ethics is that it too often ignores the fact that human beings are psychological beings. The reason why we sometimes break a moral rule is not because we do not have the proper moral philosophy in place in our head. It is because we are so fractured and immature psychologically that we cannot even come close to being able to think and act ethically. It is as if we are first graders who are being asked to read and comprehend Kant's *Groundwork of the Metaphysics of Morals*.

Ethics should be about helping the human race to become more mature, which necessitates understanding ourselves psychologically. As long as we try to do "ethics" as a philosophical exercise that ignores the empirical reality of human beings as they are, we will be wasting our time. In order to do ethics well, I am arguing, you also have to do psychology well. You have to do psychology first, so that your ethical reflections about how to make the human race better have a basis in clear understanding.

But we need to take a step back even from psychology. The *source*, the *origin*, the *starting point* for ethics is the vertical axis, which points to God. The horizontal is *not* the starting point for ethics. It is a mystery how anyone could seriously consider that possibility in the wake of the Holocaust.[47] Selfhood is also *not* the starting point for ethics. As selves we need to learn to become ethical as a life task; we do not start off with ethical maturity as our default setting. If we did, humanity would have no problems at all; there would be no oppression, violence, egotism, etc.

The proper starting point for ethical reflection is the will of God.[48] As Kierkegaard says in *Works of Love*, the commandment to love God,

47. Zygmunt Bauman argues that typical social science mistakenly assumes that morality is "maintained by the operation of societal institutions" and that this assumption "failed the test" of the Holocaust badly. Bauman, *Modernity and the Holocaust*, 198.

48. Karl Barth recognizes this clearly in the second half of *Church Dogmatics*, II/2: the subject of theological ethics "is not the Word of God as it is claimed by man, but the Word of God as it claims man" (546). However, in the *Dogmatics* in general he tends to jump directly from theology to ethics, while downplaying the intermediate step (psy-

self, and neighbor does not arise in our own heart; it comes to us from above, from God, as *the royal law* (WL, 24). To become ethical as a self is to become attuned to God and one's created nature; it is to inhabit truthfully the vertical axis. Voegelin's thought places great stress on this point, as is necessary for genuine philosophical comprehension of our situation as human beings. We are ethical or unethical as selves to the extent that we are attuned to or alienated from God's will. The horizontal plane is the sphere in which this attunement or alienation is played out on the stage of history.

The Self Is in the Trinity

My argument in this book presumes the rich backdrop of Christian Trinitarian theology. I am not assuming that my reader is familiar with this background, but he or she will at least be aware that Christians have traditionally called God Father, Son, and Holy Spirit. I cannot possibly summarize the tradition and the contemporary literature on this topic within the scope of this book. For the purposes of my argument, I need only to speak in these very broad strokes to begin sketching my picture: the vertical dimension of reality points to the "maker of heaven and earth," the one Christ called "the Father"; the temporal / selfhood dimension points to Christ as the divine, ideal embodiment of what it means to be a human self living in time; the Holy Spirit inhabits the horizontal plane as the bond of love between the Father and the Son, who communicates God's love to humanity by forming and empowering the Church for the purpose of transforming human society.

In this light, it becomes apparent that the concept of the three dimensions of reality that forms the heart of this book is an updated version of Augustine's *vestigia trinitatis* ("traces of the Trinity") that are found in the human soul by virtue of our creation by the triune God in God's image. Augustine says, for example: "The love which is of God and is God is specially the Holy Spirit, through whom is spread abroad in our hearts the charity of God by which the whole Trinity makes its habitation in us."[49] He also spoke of how the human mind is composed

chology). This method has less than ideal results when it is repeated by his student, John Howard Yoder, who did not consider the psychological question regarding why human beings are violent to be worth asking in the context of *The Politics of Jesus*.

49. Augustine, *Augustine: Later Works*, 161.

of memory, reason, and will, a trio of psychological elements analogous to the divine persons. Augustine was noticing ways in which *the Trinity is in the self.* But the concept of the dimensions as I am developing it turns this idea inside out in an interesting way. Rather than focusing on the way the Trinity is in the self, we can say that *the self is in the Trinity.* The three dimensions are the milieu in which we live, the atmosphere we breathe. In Voegelin's words: "Things do not happen in the astrophysical universe; the universe, together with all things founded in it, happens in God" (CWEV, 17:408). Voegelin is echoing the apostle Paul: "[in God] we live and move and have our being" (Acts 17:28). Given that God is triune and that God is the Creator of the world, it follows that the world is saturated with God's triune presence. Human experience is the place where the triunity of God becomes luminous when the human soul participates in the life of God.[50] Theologian Robert Jenson has helpfully developed this idea in his small but important book *On Thinking the Human.* He argues that consciousness is not something we *have* as isolated individuals; it is an event we *participate in* as creatures of God and as members of a human community.[51]

The structure of the dimensions gives us a perspective on the divine persons. René Girard is harshly critical, for example, of the notion that God is wrathful and violent, always demanding appeasement (TH, 182). We can recognize now that this image of God does not come down

50. Terrence Sherry says: "Since humans (indeed, since all creatures) live in the overlap of natural, historical and communal existence, there is no time at which they do not experience the full Trinitarian presence of the one God." *The Christo-Morphic Hermeneutical Theology of H. Richard Niebuhr*, 213. Jim Fodor offers this helpful articulation: "Indeed, because the fellowship of Father, Son, and Spirit is distinguished by continuous self-dispossession and self-giving, a certain space is opened up whereby we, as God's creatures, are enabled to share in God's Trinitarian life." He makes this comment in an essay in which he argues that Girard's thought is insufficiently Trinitarian. Fodor, "Christian Discipleship as Participative Imitation," 257–58. Thomas Smail's essay "In the Image of the Triune God" also develops the concept that the *imago dei* needs to be interpreted in Trinitarian terms. He expanded the article into a book, *Like Father, Like Son: The Trinity Imaged in Our Humanity.*

51. Jenson, *On Thinking the Human*, 28. Jenson draws on patristic thought, such as *Gregory of Nyssa's Treatise on the Inscriptions of the Psalms*, 90–91: "If, then, the orderly arrangement of the cosmos as a whole is a musical harmony, '*whose designer and maker is God,*' as the apostle says, and man is a miniature cosmos, and this same man has also been made an image of the one who composed the cosmos, what reason knows in the case of the great cosmos, this, in all likelihood, it sees also in the miniature, for the part of the whole is of the same kind in all respects as the whole."

from above as a genuine revelation of God's own nature; rather, it is an image that arises out of the horizontal dimension when it is dominated by the scapegoat mechanism. It is a projection, a form of idolatry, a volcanic eruption of human wrath shooting up into the sky. With apologies to Jonathan Edwards, this is "God in the Hands of Angry Sinners." In contrast, an authentic understanding of God the Father realizes that God is infinitely creative, seeking the flourishing of his creatures. The desire of the Creator is not for judgment and destruction but for the protection of human lives and the protection of the created environment. In the Son, Jesus Christ, we come to know God as gracious and redemptive. Jesus teaches us how to live in time through grace as we are converted away from our past enslavement to sin and guilt and our spirits are opened up to a new future walking in the light of God's forgiveness. Through the work of the Holy Spirit, the Giver of Life, we come to know God as love and as the power of social transformation in human history. The Spirit is the power of God disentangling us from the destructive web of the social scapegoating mechanism into which we are born. In Girard's words, "the Spirit is necessary in history to work to disintegrate the world and gradually discredit all the gods of violence" (TS, 207).

The argument that I have been presenting for the last few pages is overly simplistic. I have been connecting the Father with the vertical, the Son with selfhood, and the Spirit with the horizontal. But one of the key concepts in traditional theology is that "the works of the Trinity are undivided." This means that whatever the Father is doing, the Son and Spirit are doing also; whatever the Son is doing, the Father and the Spirit are doing also; whatever the Spirit is doing, the Father and the Son are doing also. We thus need to nuance the concept of the dimensions by noting that the Father is also in the selfhood dimension as the originating source of personal identity ("I am who I am"), and in the horizontal dimension as the ultimate source of love between persons.[52] The Spirit also inhabits the vertical dimension as the revealing presence of God to humanity in the inspiration of the scriptures and inhabits the temporal trajectory of selfhood as the prophetic, transforming presence of God in human history. Christ embodies the three dimensions as King, Prophet, and Priest.

52. On this topic, see James Alison's chapter on "Jesus' fraternal relocation of God" in *Faith Beyond Resentment*.

Christ is King, Prophet, and Priest

One of the key christological concepts in the history of Christian thought is the Threefold Office: Christ is King, Prophet, and Priest. When we consider this idea in relation to the three dimensions of reality we can see that it is yet another refraction of the same principles. Christ as *King* clearly fits within the vertical axis, which evokes rule, authority, majesty, higher-and-lower. The vertical axis points to the hierarchy of being with nature at the bottom and God at the top. In this dimension, Christ is the Incarnate One, God made flesh, to bring to earth the kingly rule of God. Christ is the true human being, the God-man, who lives in between God and nature, heaven and earth. He speaks with authority and heals with divine power. As *Prophet*, Christ is the teacher and guide of fallen humanity. Through his prophetic preaching, he teaches us what it means to live in time by giving us that essential form of lucidity that comes from awareness of our sin and of its forgiveness by God.[53] He enables us to live within the trajectory of selfhood with hope rather than despair by calling us to imitate him as he lived before God and for others. In his priestly role, Christ is the one who is at the same time the *Priest* and the Lamb who is slain. The Eastern Orthodox liturgy expresses this perfectly when it chants: "it is Thou who offerest and Thou who art offered . . ." This aspect of his work inhabits the horizontal plane, the home of the scapegoat mechanism. Christ allows himself to become the victim of the lynch mob to show that humanity does not need to constitute itself as a lynch mob. He adopts the role of the Priest to show that God does not require "burnt offerings and sacrifices."

If we present these concepts visually, we have another version of our diagram:

53. "Contrition is the specifically Christian form of lucidity." Bailie, *Violence Unveiled*, 40.

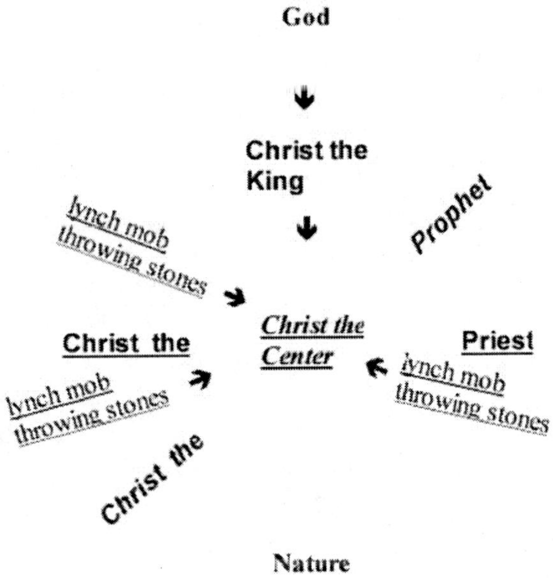

In this chart, the "lynch mob throwing stones" is to be understood as an aspect of the horizontal plane. This is a visual summary of Girard's Christology. To say that "Christ was crucified, not stoned" is to be overly literalistic. The principle is that his contemporaries insisted on killing him, by any means. Christ's kingly and prophetic roles are also present in his death. The synthesis of these roles is summarized in the phrase "Christ the Center." This is, of course, an allusion to a book by Dietrich Bonhoeffer, which I recommend to you for further exploration of these themes.

Consider this quotation from H. Richard Niebuhr:

> The cross in history may be compared to the kind of an event which an astronomer means when, having computed the positions of the planets with the aid of his excellent Ptolemaean wisdom he discovers a planet in a position that does not fit into the scheme. His whole wisdom is called into question, and eventually the Copernican or Einsteinian revolution of his science

> may result. So the cross as a simple event calls into question the foundations of our worldly wisdom.[54]

My way of presenting this idea is to assert that the New Copernican Revolution that we need is a Christological revolution. In other words, we will develop an understanding of our internal spiritual worlds as human beings when we learn from Christ what it means to be a human being. This is the unanimous conclusion of the true scientists of the spirit: Kierkegaard, Voegelin, and Girard. Girard speaks of "the unity of novelistic conclusions," by which he means that literary geniuses such as Cervantes, Flaubert, and Dostoevsky all point to the event of genuine spiritual conversion as the high point of their depictions of the human condition (DDN, 293). Changing this image slightly, we can call the symphonic insights of Kierkegaard, Voegelin, and Girard "the unity of anthropological comprehension." We will next survey how Voegelin illumines Christ the King, how Kierkegaard illumines Christ the Prophet, and how Girard illumines Christ the Priest.

Voegelin comments on Aquinas' question "Utrum Christus sit caput omnium hominum," "whether Christ is the head of all men":[55]

> What is the significance of the appearance of Christ and of his incarnation as a historical event? It means that, in the sense of Thomas, the presence under God, and the presence of God in the world, which up to then was available to men only in a profoundly ineffable form, was differentiated through the incarnation and became historically clear. Thus the whole of mankind can become retrospectively included in the incarnation as a historic event, and all of mankind is a member of the *corpus mysticum* in the sense of inclusion in God, as he realizes himself in history. And this holds similarly for the entire future. (CWEV, 31: 202–3)

He continues:

> In this historical process of increasing transparency for the central problem of order, Christianity takes a special place, insofar as in it, through the symbolism of the incarnation, the presence of God in man in society and in history is thoroughly formulated. That happened nowhere else. Only in terms of this problematic of incarnation, which then had as a consequence the

54. Niebuhr, *Theology, History, and Culture*, 205.

55. Aquinas, *Summa Theologiae* IIIa.8.3.

> whole problematic of the Trinity and the dogma of the Trinity, is it unequivocally said what man is. That is to say, man is man insofar as he is *imago Dei*, and insofar as he is *imago Dei* are all men equal as participating in the reality of God and thus united with God, who historically has become flesh in the process of history. This is precisely what is characteristic of Christianity, its unique achievement. Every attempt to withdraw from this achievement is a regression in differentiation and an attempt to reintroduce more compact ideas of the existence of man and of his order. (CWEV, 31: 204–5)

Voegelin sums up his reflections along these lines in the phrase "history is Christ written large" (CWEV, 12: 78). He means that in Christ we see human existence revealed most clearly as the experience of living *in-between* (in-between time and eternity, nature and God). This reality of the in-between was expressed by the Definition of Chalcedon in 451 with its language of the two natures of Christ held together in indissoluble unity. "The reality of the Mediator and the intermediate reality of [human] consciousness have the same structure" (CWEV, 12: 79).

The secondary literature on Voegelin contains a large amount of hand-wringing over the relationship between Voegelin and Christianity. Certain Christian scholars who comment on him are hesitant to state that he is a Christian, or that he is theologically orthodox. While I do not mean to belittle this literature and the serious questions that it asks, it strikes me that the concerns may be overdone. If ever there was a case where the cliché that "all truth is God's truth" applies, it is here. Voegelin may have been more of a Platonic than a New Testament theologian, but his vision of the sources of truth is so clear and penetrating that his articulation of biblical and patristic truths far outstrips that of many more pedestrian theologians whose orthodoxy is never questioned. As I have been arguing in this book, Voegelin is primarily a vertical axis thinker, meaning that his awareness of the prophetic-christological dimension is not quite as subtle as Kierkegaard's, and his awareness of the priestly-horizontal dimension is not quite as subtle as Girard's. But from my point of view, this need not be a cause for hand-wringing. One can appreciate and affirm Voegelin's achievement in this broader and more complex frame of reference.[56]

56. For substantive reflections on the relation between Voegelin and Girard, see Ranieri, "What Voegelin Missed in the Gospel." Ranieri tends to argue that we must

~

Kierkegaard's thought focuses intently on the selfhood dimension of existence. In this dimension, Christ is the Prototype, the model of what it means to be a human being. But we human beings do not want to become human beings. This is the central paradox of our fallen condition. In Christ's life on this earth, the spiritual demand placed on human beings to grow toward maturity was ratcheted up to the highest possible level:

> A self directly before Christ is a self intensified by the inordinate concession from God, intensified by the inordinate accent that falls upon it because God allowed himself to be born, become man, suffer, and die also for the sake of this self. As stated previously, the greater the conception of God, the more self; so it holds true here: the greater the conception of Christ, the more self. Qualitatively a self is what its criterion is. That Christ is the criterion is the expression, attested by God, for the staggering reality that a self has, for only in Christ is it true that God is man's goal and criterion, or the criterion and goal. —But the more self there is, the more intense is sin. (SUD, 113–14)

Kierkegaard's awareness of human rejection of the call of creation is unsurpassed by any other thinker that I am aware of. But he does not give up hope for humanity and become darkly pessimistic. He is always hopeful, pointing to God's unchanging grace and love toward humanity.

Kierkegaard offered deep reflections on John 12:32 "And I, when I am lifted up from the earth, will draw all to myself." He argued that earthly things that are empty and perishing cannot draw to themselves, except in a deceptive way. Only God, who is the highest and most real reality, can "draw" in the true sense. And this is precisely what God does through Christ; he draws human beings up into the fullness of what it means to be a human being:

> So, then, what truly can be said to draw to itself must be something in itself or something that is in itself. So it is when truth draws to itself, for truth is in itself, is in and for itself—and Christ is the truth. It must be the higher that draws the lower

---

place our allegiance with one of the two thinkers. My approach in this book is obviously different, in that I seek to notice the different emphases of the thinkers and combine their strengths.

> to itself—just as when Christ, the infinitely highest one, true God and true man, from on high will draw all to himself. But the human being of whom this discourse speaks is in himself a self. Therefore Christ also first and foremost wants to help every human being to become a self, requires this of him first and foremost, requires that he, by repenting, become a self, in order then to draw him to himself. He wants to draw the human being to himself, but in order truly to draw him to himself he wants to draw him only as a free being to himself, that is, through a choice. (PC, 159–60)

We see here how Kierkegaard expresses Christ's role as Prophet so powerfully. The Prophet is not a predictor of future events, but one who continually calls human beings to turn from the errant path they have chosen for themselves in defiance of God; the Prophet calls us to choose rightly, which means to walk in the reality that we have already been chosen by God's grace to be God's children.

~

René Girard also presents a perspective on Christ the Center. He argues that the center of human culture is constituted by violence directed toward scapegoats. Christ places himself in that center to reveal it, to expose it to the light of day. In this way Christ is the true Priest who mediates between God and humanity:

> To recognize Christ as God is to recognize him as the only being capable of rising above the violence that had, up to that point, absolutely transcended humankind. Violence is the controlling agent in every form of mythic or cultural structure, and Christ is the only agent who is capable of escaping from these structures and freeing us from their dominance . . . A non-violent deity can only signal his existence to humankind by having himself driven out by violence—by demonstrating that he is not able to establish himself in the Kingdom of Violence. (TH, 219)

It is common in the Christian tradition to think of Christ as a sacrifice offered to God the Father to appease His wrath toward sinners. Girard's thought shows the theological inadequacy of this view. It is we human beings who are wrathful; God is offering His Son to appease us. Christ reveals God, meaning that God is not wrathful but loving:

> Jesus is the only man who achieves the goal God has set for all mankind, the only man who has nothing to do with violence

> and its works. The epithet 'Son of Man' also corresponds, quite clearly, to the fact that Jesus alone has fulfilled a calling that belongs to all mankind.
>
> If the fulfillment, on earth, passes inevitably through the death of Jesus, this is not because the Father demands this death, for strange sacrificial motives. Neither the son nor the Father should be questioned about the cause of this event, but all mankind, and mankind alone. The very fact that mankind has never really managed to understand what is involved reveals clearly that the misunderstanding of the founding murder is still being perpetuated, as is our inability to hear the Word of God. (TH, 213)

Like Kierkegaard, Girard is also optimistic about human beings despite the obvious depths of our depravity and violence. We always have the potential to escape from the death trap of mimetic desire and become individual human subjects. Instead of imitating the models of our culture that lead to rivalry and conflict, we can imitate Christ:

> The gospel text, especially John but also to a certain extent the synoptic Gospels, establish beyond any doubt the fact that Jesus is both God and Man. The theology of the Incarnation is not just a fantastic and irrelevant invention of the theologians; it adheres rigorously to the logic implicit in the text. But it only succeeds in becoming intelligible if we read the text in non-sacrificial rather than sacrificial terms. This is, in effect, the only time that this notion of a fullness of humanity that is also a fullness of divinity makes sense in a context that is as 'humanist' as it is 'religious'. If Jesus is the only one who can fully reveal the way in which the founding murder has broadened its hold upon mankind, this is because at no point did it take hold upon him. Jesus explains to us mankind's true vocation, which is to throw off the hold of the founding murder. (TH, 216)

A hymn says that "the Lamb is the light of the city of God."[57] This clustering of images drawn from the book of Revelation serves well as a summary of Girard's analysis of human culture. We need to emphasize that for Girard, the city of God is not an abstract, transcendental notion of the afterlife. The world in which we live *is* the city of God, and the light, Christ, *is* shining in it.

57. "I Want to Walk As a Child of the Light," words by Kathleen Thomerson.

Atonement Is At-Three-ment

Atonement is a hot topic in theology these days. The fact that there have been many books written on this doctrine recently suggests that we are at a hinge point in the history of Christian thought.[58] The authors of these books realize that the stakes are high, because atonement is not simply one Christian doctrine, it is *the* Christian doctrine. In other words, all of the traditional doctrines (creation, sin, anthropology, Christology, ecclesiology, etc.) either flow into or flow out of the dominant understanding of atonement that is at work in a particular theological worldview. If the penal substitution view of atonement, for example, comes under heavy criticism from various directions, its adherents feel that they must defend it successfully, or their theological house will come crashing down; those who attack that view believe that they are escaping from a nightmare of primitive thinking and charting the pathway to a brand new type of Christian theology for the future.

Many pages in books about atonement are spent discussing the different types of atonement theories that have been put forward in the history of Christian thought. Some theories are God-oriented, focusing on satisfaction of God's honor or justice; some are human-oriented, focusing on how we are changed subjectively by viewing the Cross; some are Satan-oriented, focusing on how the Cross was a victory that released humanity from bondage to the demonic principalities and powers. Each of these perspectives can draw on passages in the Bible, which is of course another major topic of discussion in these books. A complete discussion of this topic is far beyond the scope of this book, but reflections on the contributions of Mark Heim (*Saved from Sacrifice: A Theology of the Cross*) and Robert Sherman (*King, Priest, and Prophet: A Trinitarian Theology of Atonement*) will set up an opportunity to present my own reflections on why there are different theories of atonement at all, and on why the doctrine of the Trinity is the key to this puzzle.

In my view, Heim's book is superb. He takes up the task of thinking through the doctrine of atonement in the wake of René Girard's anthropological theory. Girard himself is hesitant to speak as a "theologian," though he does make positive comments about the "victory over the devil" theory in his book *I See Satan Fall Like Lightning* (137–53). Heim

58. I am referring to Western Christian thought, which is much less stable than Eastern Orthodoxy.

is a first-rate theological thinker, and his achievement in *Saved from Sacrifice* is that he articulates the theological implications of Girard's thought more effectively than Girard is able to do himself. This enables Heim to explain in a compelling way what it means to say that the execution of Christ was the sacrifice to end all sacrifices.

Saved from Sacrifice has three main phases in its argument. In the first phase, Heim summarizes Girard's notion of the invisibility of scapegoats as the starting point for human cultural formation. Cultures come into existence through an act of scapegoating that allows the members of the society to channel their violence toward a victim as a way of avoiding generalized chaos. But the society will not remember the act of scapegoating as an act of scapegoating—as something arbitrary and thus morally wrong. They will instead tell a story that justifies their actions by depicting the one killed as deserving to die. From the point of view of the Roman and Jewish authorities who wanted to get rid of Jesus, his death was simply another example of such a deserved death.

The second phase of the argument focuses on the Bible's revelation of unconscious scapegoating. By taking the side of the victim in certain key passages in Genesis, the Psalms, Isaiah, Job, and the Gospels, the biblical revelation unmasks the violent mechanism of cultural formation. Human culture wants to remain blissfully unconscious, but the Bible refuses to let it do so. The Bible awakens us at the same time that it convicts us. The first and second phases of Heim's argument are summarized in this passage: "In the self-perception of those who practice scapegoating sacrifice, there is no awareness that any injustice or sin is being committed by the community. The writers of the Gospels not only make it clear that evil is being done. They make it clear that the community that does it includes them."[59] The Holy Spirit is traditionally thought of as the inspirer of the scriptures. This fits perfectly with the understanding of the Holy Spirit that arises out of Girard's thought and is fleshed out so well by Heim. The Holy Spirit is the Paraclete, the attorney for the defense who is continually countering the work of Satan, the accuser, the whisperer-behind-the-lynch-mob.

The third phase of Heim's argument concerns the practical implications of the second phase. Given that the Bible unveils the roots of cultural violence, where does that leave us? How does this knowl-

59. Heim, *Saved from Sacrifice*, 118.

edge become more than just knowledge? How can it change the world? The Church is the practical outworking of the biblical revelation. The Church is the place where Christ's sacrifice to end all sacrifices becomes the chief teaching and the pulsing Eucharistic heart. The Church is the community that turns the violent world inside out, making possible a different pattern for individual psychology and social politics. To speak in this way about the Church is obviously idealistic; we are describing the *ideal* of what the Church should be. In the actual course of history, Christians as individuals and the Church as a body have often reverted to violent, sacrificial behavior. Heim is fully aware of that, and his book actually functions as a very effective Girardian commentary on the history of Christianity. But just because the Church has failed to embody the ideal does not mean that the ideal does not exist. The ideal is always present to us, beckoning us forward, reforming us, transforming us. We can always hope that the Church will move closer to the ideal in the future, and that its movement away from violence will serve as a contagious model for the world at large, transforming human culture.

Heim says that the "problem with most traditional language about Christ's death is not that it is wrong, but that it balances on a knife's edge of interpretation."[60] To say that "Christ died for us," for example, can have very different meanings on the lips of three different individuals. One person might say: "Christ died for us. He was stabbed in the back by those Christ-killing Jews. Therefore we should make the world a better place by killing all the Jews." Another person might say: "Christ died for us. He absorbed within himself the outpouring of the Father's wrath toward sin so that we could be let off the hook and avoid going to hell." Another person might say: "Christ died for us. He placed himself in the middle of the lynch mob so that we human beings could come to understand our sickness. He became our victim so that we could learn to live without victimizing each other any longer." The achievement of Heim's book is to place the traditional language of piety within a context that makes such differing interpretations understandable, while showing that the third view is the one that is most faithful to the deep grammar of the Christian faith.

60. Ibid., 306.

~

In 1931 Gustaf Aulén published a book entitled: *Christus Victor: An Historical Study of the Three Main Types of the Idea of Atonement.* His manner of laying out the Anselmian satisfaction theory, the moral influence theory, and the ransom, or "victory over the devil," theory has been widely influential in Christian reflection on atonement in recent decades. The Girardian theory, as developed by Heim, is clearly an example of the "victory over the devil" theory, with the devil being understood as the scapegoat mechanism of cultural formation. Robert Sherman has written a book (*King, Priest, and Prophet: A Trinitarian Theology of Atonement*) that approaches the same topic that Aulen approached, but with an interesting question in mind: Why are there three main types of atonement theory? Sherman's intuition, which drives his book, is that there are different types because reality, as it has been created by God, is threefold, and this threefoldness is a reflection of the triune nature of God. I judge Sherman's instincts along these lines to be correct, though I have a different perspective on how to parse the threefoldness.

Sherman develops his intuition by seeking to correlate three sets of threes: God as Father, Son, and Holy Spirit; the offices of Christ (king, priest, and prophet); and the three main types of atonement theory. This creates a tic-tac-toe board, which Sherman fills in this way:[61]

Father	Son	Holy Spirit
King	Priest	Prophet
Victory over Satan	Satisfaction	Moral influence

His project requires him to explain why he has arranged the lower two rows in the manner he did. Why is priest under Son and prophet under Spirit, rather than vice versa? Why are the atonement theories placed where they are? He explains his reasoning in this way:

> (First column) "... our context must be redeemed from the powers that hold it in thrall before the next two models of atonement would 'work' or even make sense. Christ's victory over the principalities and powers reclaims creation, which is to say, the

61. Sherman, *King, Priest, and Prophet*, 23.

'natural,' and those born from a now fallen nature, for God the Father's original purposes."[62]

(Second column) "... in accord with the loving and righteous will of God the Father, God the Son freely takes on flesh by means of God the Spirit to become Christ the priest and sacrifice, to atone for human sin and restore creation to right relation with God and its own integrity. In this work, one may recognize Christ's priestly work of atonement as the work appropriate to the Son ... God the Son takes to himself this role, he becomes Christ the Priest, in order to reconcile a sinful humanity to God's holiness. He takes on human flesh to serve as humanity's representative and priest, because it is humanity that stands in need of making sacrifice to God."[63]

(Third column) "Given the unfolding logic of my project, it may be obvious why I believe this aspect of Christ's atoning work should be considered third: there is a soteriological correspondence to the theological place of the Holy Spirit 'after' the Father and the Son. To use a farming metaphor, the ground must be prepared to receive the gift of the Spirit. That is, now that the principalities and powers have been defeated, now that the pollution of human sin and guilt has been washed away, the new creation can take root and grow. This aspect of the Messiah's work is accomplished through the outpouring of the Holy Spirit. Moreover, the Spirit represents and is the effective agent of God's eschatological future. As Christ the King's work served to reclaim creation from its past bondage for the Father's original intentions, as Christ the Priest's work served to reclaim, indeed, establish a free and truly open present, so, too, does Christ the Prophet's work proclaim and serve the in-breaking power of God's intended future for humanity and all creation."[64]

Sherman's book is weighty and substantive. It is obviously the result of many years of reading and reflection. He has good reasons to argue as he does; my thumbnail summary of his argument does not do it justice. However, it is interesting to note that I had the same original intuition that Sherman had, yet I came to different conclusions about how the columns should be organized. Of course, in my own eyes my arrange-

62. Ibid., 159–60.

63. Ibid., 210.

64. Ibid., 250–51.

ment makes as much sense if not more sense than his. This situation illustrates the complexity of Trinitarian theology.

I first became aware of Sherman's book after I had already set myself the same task, to correlate the three sets of threes. But my way of filling in the tic-tac-toe board was very different from Sherman's:

Father	Son	Holy Spirit
King	Prophet	Priest
Satisfaction	Moral influence	Victory over Satan

The three traditional types of atonement theories are God-oriented, human-oriented, and Satan-oriented. They seek to answer the question: Who is changed in the event that we call "atonement"? Is it God who is changed by being "satisfied"? Is it we who are changed psychologically? Is it Satan who is changed by being dethroned as the false head of humanity? When we put it in these terms, we can see an alternative to Sherman's schema. If God the Father is being changed by satisfaction, then that theory would have to go in the first column. It would also make sense to put the moral influence theory in the Son column, because we are being changed into the image of Christ as we behold his divine love for us. I placed the victory over Satan theory in the Holy Spirit column because my thinking, like Heim's, is very much influenced byRené Girard. Girard argues that Satan is the Accuser, the prosecuting attorney who is always seeking to encourage human cultures to gang up on scapegoats. The Holy Spirit is the Paraclete, the defense attorney whose work is to unveil Satan's schemes by vindicating scapegoats. I placed Christ's role as Prophet in the Son column because the Prophet speaks to human beings and calls them to repentance; this was Christ's ministry before and leading up to the Cross. On the Cross, Christ was performing the Priestly role. He was the Lamb who was slain at the same time as he was the High Priest who was bringing human sacrifice to an end. This lines up perfectly with what I was just saying about the Paraclete. Girard's thought shows that Christ placed himself in the middle of the lynch mob so that the lynch mob would be undermined from that point forward in history. This picture is rounded out by noting the one place I agree with Sherman's chart. Christ the King goes in the Father column; this points to Christ's role as Healer, as the one who brings creation to completion. It also points to Christ's headship over the human race from the beginning to the end of time as the Word through whom all things came into being.

Sherman is working with the assumption that there must be some truth in each of the three types; thus, the task is to hold the types in a creative tension within a Trinitarian framework. In his words: "unlike Aulen's approach, I do not offer three models in order to critique two and advocate the third. Rather, I see my three as complementing and completing one another."[65] I have a somewhat different view, in the sense that I have no desire to defend the satisfaction theory in any of its variations. When I place it in the "Father" column I am simply noting that it fits there because it is a God-the-Father-oriented theory, but this says nothing about its theological soundness. It could be based on a false image of who the Father is, as I do in fact believe it is. My case here is supported by pointing out that Christian fundamentalists, who tend to be *patriarchal* (Father-oriented), favor this view of atonement and make it the controlling center of every evangelistic sermon.

The second point of divergence is that my reflections on the topic of atonement are one aspect of a much larger project of theological anthropology that I am developing. (Sherman's tic-tac-toe chart takes up about half of one page in his book. When I became aware of Sherman's book, I had already developed a much more comprehensive chart that I had to print on *both sides* of an 11 x 17 piece of paper.)[66] This larger vision establishes the overall framework for the particular issue of atonement. I am suggesting an approach that weaves together atonement, the Trinity, and theological anthropology (understood as an empirically oriented interpretation of observable personality types). This aspect shows the strong influence of Girard on me, which tunes theology in a social scientific key.

~

The word "atonement" is a construction within the history of the English language, coined by William Tyndale, drawing on the image of being

65. Ibid., 20.

66. The online version is here: "The Trinity, Human Psychology, and Theological Method." http://tinyurl.com/yron7g.

made "at one" with another from whom one is alienated. It is used theologically to indicate the reconciliation that occurs between God and human beings in the event of salvation. The particular contribution to the discussion that I can offer here is a neologism, which I sincerely hope no one will repeat after me: atonement is *at-three-ment*. In other words, what does it mean to be made *at one* with a God who is *at three*? What does atonement mean in relation to the three dimensions of reality that we have been considering throughout this book?

Jesus put it as succinctly as it can be put: we are to love God, our selves, and our neighbor. This sums up the Law and the Prophets. To love God is to receive God's grace that transforms us and sustains us. To love our selves is the opposite of narcissism; it is a recognition that we flourish *with* others, not *against* them. To love my neighbors is to value their well-being and flourishing just as I value my own.

The apostle Paul also put it very succinctly in his famous triad: faith, hope, and love. Faith is the openness of the human spirit to God; its upward movement echoes the downward movement of grace. Hope lives into the future in the confidence that the ultimate ground of reality is God's life, not our death. Love is attunement with God's desire that all human beings live at peace with themselves and with others. Love hopes for the opening up of faith in the neighbor. Love recognizes that to love the neighbor we must be the neighbor by redoubling the reality that God has chosen to be our neighbor in Christ.[67]

Faith, hope, and love point to the vertical axis, the future, and the horizontal plane, but what about the portion of the temporal trajectory that we call the past? Here, the appropriate virtue is that wisdom that comes from recognizing that truth is accumulative. Fundamentalism wants to travel backward in a time machine to a Golden Age in the past. Modern individualism and Marxist utopianism both tend to dismiss the past as backwardness and superstition. All three of these forms of contracted existence resist the idea that truth is accumulative. To grow as human beings, we need to study the past, to gather from it the wisdom that has been articulated in the scriptures and in the religious tradition leading up to our day. When we allow this wisdom to accumulate within us and shape our consciousness, we are being brought into existence as God's children. The fullness of time enters into us—past, present, and

67. I am summarizing Kierkegaard's *Works of Love* in a tiny nutshell.

future. We do not "know" and "critique" as isolated individuals from a position of absolute rest, but as participants in motion in a great stream of being that is so much larger than ourselves.[68]

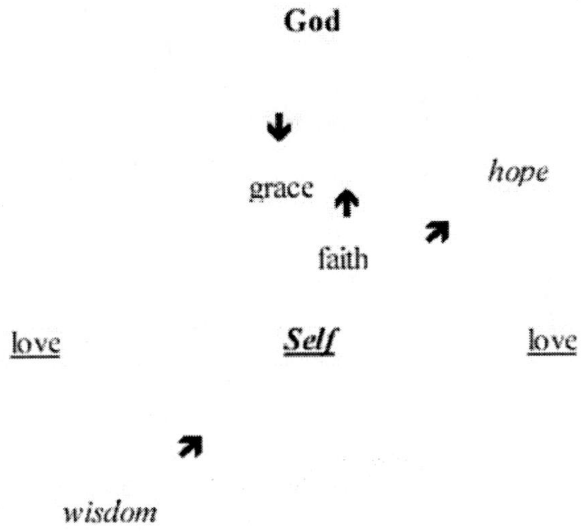

The maturing person who inhabits the theological virtues lives in openness to the ongoing event of creation that is happening within and around the self. This personality type does not arrogantly seek to seize control of the event of creation, as the utopian does. He or she is active in seeking to transform the world, but in cooperation with God, not in defiance of God. To be *active* in the right way, one must first have been *receptive* of God's grace.

The maturing person enacts the true meaning of the word *freedom*, which is tossed around so thoughtlessly in our age. Genuine freedom is not "the ability to do whatever I want," but the ability to do what is best for myself and for the neighbor by being attuned to God's desires for human redemption. This can be called "freedom for excellence" as distinct from the "freedom of indifference" that we modern Westerners often think is the apex of human evolution.[69] In sum, *to be made one*

68. See Torrance, *Theological Science*, 154, where he compares Kierkegaard with Einstein, "who made such an immense advance through abandoning the conception of space and time reached from a point of absolute rest."

69. For a thorough expansion of this point, in conversation with Thomas Aquinas, see Pinckaers, *The Sources of Christian Ethics*. The same author has also produced a

with the God who is triune is to be opened up to existence in the fullness of the three dimensions of reality.

My reader will have noted that I have avoided talking about the crucial thing, the Cross of Christ. How does it save us? To this question I will simply respond by saying: read Heim's book; it is superb. The "victory over the devil" theory as modified by Girard's anthropology is the correct way to interpret the crucifixion of Christ. The "atonement is at-three-ment" theory that I have just outlined can be understood as supplementing this view of the cross with a vision of how we are changed by God in the event of redemption. This is an updated version of the Eastern Orthodox "recapitulation" view of salvation, which has been articulated in this way by Alexander Schmemann:

> There must be someone in this world—which rejected God and in this rejection, in this blasphemy, became a chaos of darkness—there must be someone to stand in its center, and to discern, to see it again as full of divine riches, as the cup full of life and joy, as beauty and wisdom, and to thank God for it. This "someone" is Christ, the new Adam who restores that "eucharistic life" which I, the old Adam, have rejected and lost; who makes me again what I am, and restores the world to me. And if the Church *is in Christ*, its initial act is always this act of thanksgiving, of returning the world to God.[70]

concise version: *Morality: The Catholic View*.

70. Schmemann, *For the Life of the World*, 60–61. David Hart amplifies this thought: "Salvation occurs by way of recapitulation, the restoration of the human image in Christ, the eternal image of the Father after whom humanity was created in the beginning; thus salvation consists in the recovery of a concrete form, and in the restoration of an original beauty." *The Beauty of the Infinite*, 318. Sin is understood by Hart as human rejection of this true form: "In entering into a world that has fallen under the power of principalities whose rule is violence and lies, the true human pattern (the Logos) can appear only as a form crucified, which the world can grasp only as contrariety. Nonetheless, it is a real form, it assumes palpable shape within time, it can be beheld, imitated, obeyed, and adored; in Christ a real reversal has occurred, within historical experience, a real and visible beauty has cast its light upon the figure of sinful humanity and revealed it to be a false image, an apostasy of the soul from its own beauty." *The Beauty of the Infinite*, 326. Glenn Tinder makes a similar argument, but with a forward-looking emphasis: "The divine transfiguration of our lives—lives carried on in time—is a reshaping of human destiny in response to sin. The principal condition of destiny, as I have argued, is not sin but freedom; because we are free, our glory as creatures of God, and the only creatures made in God's image, is not possessed as a natural characteristic

Schmemann's argument here is similar to Karl Barth's interpretation of Romans 5:

> Christ stands above and is first, and Adam stands below and is second. So it is Christ that reveals the true nature of man. Man's nature in Adam is not, as is usually assumed, his true and original nature; it is only truly human at all in so far as it reflects and corresponds to essential human nature as it is found in Christ. True human nature, therefore, can only be understood by Christians who look to Christ to discover the essential nature of man.[71]

These quotations express well the basic presupposition of the Christian social science that I have been seeking to articulate in this book. If we wish to engage in real anthropological interpretation, it will not work to look at human beings in general; we need a touchstone, a key, a central image that enables us to comprehend true human nature and its false pathologies. Christ is that touchstone. When we are made *at one* with the God who is *at three*, then our eyes are opened up to see the true human image.

~

The view of atonement that assumes that a stream of violence flowing from God was diverted from the human race to Christ is no longer plausible, in my view. Millard Erickson, for example, says: "God would not have gone so far as to put his precious Son to death had it not been absolutely necessary."[72] There is a dual mistake being made in this type of thinking: (1) Christ's death is seen as caused by God the Father rather than by the Roman and Jewish leaders who were enacting the scapegoat mechanism, and (2) the unquestioning adoption of an image of a (violent) God that is the product of (violent) human culture. Erickson's version of logic forces him to believe that because Jesus had to be sacrificed to appease the Father, therefore the Father made the Roman and Jewish leaders crucify him; this was an evil act, which makes the Father

but must be deliberately affirmed. In this way the glory of our divine likeness is given to us as something that lies before us, in the future. But we have rejected the future thus put before us and cast aside the divine likeness offered us. This is our primal sin—the refusal of our original destiny." *The Political Meaning of Christianity*, 42–43.

71. Barth, *Christ and Adam*, 112.

72. Erickson, *Christian Theology*, 840.

the ultimate author of evil. Our task today is to realize that God is not a wrathful judge who must be appeased through blood sacrifices. In Heim's words: "God did not become human only to die . . . Anselm's doctrine preserves the paradox, but the wrong one. He has made the cross a celebration of the sacrifice it meant to overcome."[73] The correct way of thinking about God along the vertical axis is not God as sacred executioner of God's Son, but rather God as loving and gracious Creator of the human race who sent the Son to release us from our *self-imposed* condemnation. In Karl Barth's words, which are crucially important for framing the entire topic of atonement, "God does not need reconciliation with men, but men need reconciliation with Him."[74] This is the central meaning of the parable of the Prodigal Son.

The Church Is the Place Where the New Copernican Revolution Is Incubated

As I argued above, the proper method for theological thinking is something other than simply finding the correct way of thinking. What is needed on a deeper level than thinking correctly is *existing correctly*. The choices we make deep in our souls about how we are going to exist in time shape the way we think as an aftereffect. What is needed at this basic level is a movement of soul that we can describe as *opening ourselves up to the fullness of time*. The orientation of our souls toward our source, God, and toward the milieu in which we live, time and the neighbor, will enable our thinking to gain the key elements it needs, ordered in an appropriate way. The Church, in the ideal sense, is the place where people learn how to exist correctly by learning who God is, who they are, and what they should do and say to make a transforming impact on the world. When Christian theology is on track in the Church, it teaches that God is not a bloodthirsty deity requiring appeasement, but the loving Creator of a *good* creation. The Son, Jesus Christ, reveals to us the character and purposes of God. In Michael Ramsey's memorable words: "The importance of the confession 'Jesus is Lord' is not only that Jesus is divine but that God is Christlike. 'God is Christlike and in him is no

73. Heim, *Saved from Sacrifice*, 301. Another critique of Anselm's view of atonement has been articulated by Timothy Gorringe in *God's Just Vengeance*.

74. Barth, *Church Dogmatics*, IV/1, 74.

unChristlikeness at all.'"[75] God does not require and demand continual sacrifices on an altar. The mission of Christ to the world was to bring to an end altars and sacrifices. This is the meaning of the Eucharistic meal, when it is rightly understood. The Eucharist reminds us that Christ was killed by the world's rejection of God's grace and truth. But this meal is not a preparation for revenge; it is the ultimate defeat of the spirit of revenge, as it reveals that God is gracious and forgiving to the whole human race through the resurrection of Christ.[76]

When a person learns from Christ who God is, he or she is drawn up into the life of the Trinity. The human self becomes constituted by faith, hope, and love, by love of God, self, and neighbor. In this way, the person acquires stability and weightiness, in contrast to the thin versions of transitory selfhood that human culture's mimetic desire produces. When a community of persons with stability is formed, it takes on a character that distinguishes it from communities that are mechanisms for the promotion of self-interest. This community of persons, the Church, journeys through time and develops a tradition within which human beings are nurtured by the wisdom of the past. The sacred scriptures reveal who God is when they are interpreted rightly by this community.[77] What we are describing is, of course, the work of the Holy Spirit. The Paraclete, the attorney for the defense of humanity against the work of Satan, is the one who carries God's work of redemption forward through time. The Spirit reunites us with God by revealing to us the Son, who taught us that God desires "mercy, not sacrifice," compassion, not bloodshed. The triune God who has created the world and human beings is love. When we allow God's grace to draw us upward spiritually, we are transformed into people who love God, self, and others. In this way we embody, *as a congregation*, and *in our time and place*, the image of God.

75. Ramsey, *God, Christ, and the World*, 98.

76. A helpful discussion of the Eucharist along these lines is provided by Heim, *Saved from Sacrifice*, 231–36. See also William Cavanaugh's book, *Theopolitical Imagination*, a deep meditation on the Eucharist as a counter-politics to the state's rule through violence.

77. Those readers who are familiar with Stanley Hauerwas will realize that I am alluding to themes that he has developed extensively. See Russell Reno's excellent summary of Hauerwas in *The Blackwell Companion to Political Theology*. See also Colin Gunton's essay "The Church as a School of Virtue? Human Formation in Trinitarian Framework," in Gunton, *Intellect and Action*.

Neither Just War Nor Pacifism Is the Solution to Violence

There is a long-running debate within the history of Christian thought regarding the issue of participation in the use of force by the state. Put in overly simple terms, some Christian theologians have argued that it is appropriate for Christians to participate in the police functions of the state, and in just wars. Other theologians have argued that Christians should be pacifists, never using deadly force, even in self-defense. Both positions, with their many subtle variations, have had articulate defenders.[78] The Three Offices of Christ are relevant to this debate.

The position that accepts the use of force inhabits the vertical, kingly axis. This dimension is rooted in our bodily existence as human beings, and recognizes the need for order and structure within which human life can flourish. At its most basic, the role of the state is to keep people alive in the face of varied threats. We can see this role enacted in the work of firefighters and paramedics, and when the police are called in to stop a person who is on a rampage with a gun. In an ideal world, the police would always be able to stop such a rampage without using deadly force, but we do not live in an ideal world. When an army is called on to protect territory from invaders, the same principle is enacted on a larger scale. This strand of Christian ethics was articulated forcefully by Reinhold Niebuhr. He stressed the idea that there will always be a gap between our ideals and the fallen world within which we live. We need to accept this gap with a sense of our imperfections and the ironic situation they create for us.[79]

In the life of Christ, there is a story of an exorcism in which Christ left the demon-possessed man "clothed and in his right mind" (Luke 8:26-39). He did not simply say a prayer of hopeful blessing and then let the man continue to run amok. He took effective action to stop the mayhem. Much of what we know as police work in the modern world is analogous to this, though without the miraculous power. The police seek to the best of their ability to limit the mayhem that human beings are capable of. When this principle is expanded to the international level, the use of force to stop out-of-control violence becomes an ethical

78. The history and the arguments are capably surveyed here: Cahill, *Love Your Enemies: Discipleship, Pacifism, and Just War Theory.*

79. See Niebuhr, *An Interpretation of Christian Ethics.*

imperative to protect vulnerable human lives. An opportunity to apply this principle was provided by the situation in Rwanda in 1994. The U.N. commander, General Dallaire, said that with five thousand soldiers and a free hand to do what needed to be done, he could have stopped the genocide. But the international community did not have the will to effectively limit the mayhem; it could have.[80]

The pacifist argument has its appropriate home on the horizontal plane where we find Christ the Priest. Here, Christ allows himself to become the victim of the mob's violence without retaliating in kind. He absorbs within himself the outflow of evil from the scapegoat mechanism to expose it to the light of divine revelation, in which light the mechanism is powerless to defend itself. This dimension of reality is found at the heart of the arguments of two key Christian thinkers in recent decades: John Howard Yoder and René Girard. Yoder is the leading pacifist theologian of our age; he argues clearly and forcefully that Christ's life and death show that God's ultimate response to evil is to defeat it by absorbing it with an attitude of love toward its perpetrators. This love is transcendent, meaning that it is not concerned with calculations of worldly consequences.[81] Note the title of Yoder's main work: *The Politics of Jesus: Vicit Agnus Noster*. The Latin subtitle means "our lamb has conquered" (. . . him let us follow). Another work by Yoder is called *The Priestly Kingdom: Social Ethics as Gospel*. This emphasis on the priestly work of Christ and his followers fits well with the three offices of Christ as we have outlined them. Girard's thought provides an anthropology that corresponds well with Yoder's ethics, which accounts for the growing interest in Girard among Christian pacifists.[82] Girard

80. See Gourevitch, *We Wish to Inform You That Tomorrow We Will Be Killed with Our Families*, 150. I agree with most of what Craig Carter argues in *Rethinking Christ and Culture*, but I do not find in that book a sense that vulnerable lives should be protected in a circumstance such as Rwanda. Like his mentor, John Howard Yoder, Carter also seems to be lacking in the area of serious psychological reflection on violent behavior.

81. See Yoder, *The Politics of Jesus*, 237–39, on "accepting powerlessness."

82. See this collection of essays, for example: Swartley, ed., *Violence Renounced: Rene Girard, Biblical Studies, and Peacemaking*. See also the web sites of Paul Neuchterlein (Girardian Reflections on the Lectionary) and Michael Hardin (Preaching Peace). One should not assume that Girard himself is a pacifist; the point being made here is that his ideas are intriguing to pacifists. As far as I know, Girard is not a pacifist; he has not addressed that ethical issue directly in his writings, so it is difficult to speak more definitely. For thoughts on Girard, atonement theology, and pacifism, see George

has elucidated the workings of the horizontal plane where we find at work the satanic scapegoating mechanism and the divine unveiling of it through the Cross.

This argument between defenders of the use of force and pacifists tends to be a stalemate on the intellectual level and a landslide in favor of force on the level of how most Christians have behaved throughout most of history. The fact that most of this historical experience is infected with mimesis and scapegoating confuses the issue greatly, but that does not by itself invalidate the argument that there are some circumstances in which the use of force can actually be an expression of love of neighbor through the limitation of mayhem.

I do not view either just use of force theory or pacifism as being a "solution" to the problem of violence. The first can try to limit violence, but it cannot end it. The other can witness to God's eternal life, which is not harmed by this world's violence, but it is by definition absorptive, not an effective brake on violence. (If it were such a brake, the Nazis would have stopped killing after the millionth victim, all of sudden realizing the error of their ways.) We can see another avenue of approach to this problem in the third office: Christ as Prophet.

The only possible "solution" to the problem of violence in this world will be found in the dynamics of human spiritual transformation. If each human being, or at least a critical mass of people, were to travel down the pathway of spiritual openness to God, then the energy that currently feeds the phenomenon of violence would be drained away. Violence is driven by human rejection of the call of creation, which seeks to draw us into the future that awaits us as children birthed by the God who is Love. This rejection leads to society and culture as we know it, that culture anatomized by Girard as satanic. If we listen to the call of creation, however, we are disentangled from the violent crowd and allowed to develop our authentic selfhood as human beings. This is the work of Christ the Prophet; he calls to us, simultaneously judging and forgiving our complicity in the world's rejection of the call of creation. He frees us from the past and opens up a new future for us.

Reinhold Niebuhr, who continually warns his readers against seeking an overly narrow and "pure" vantage point, expresses well the balancing act that is needed:

Hunsinger's essay "The Politics of the Nonviolent God: Reflections on René Girard and Karl Barth," in *Disruptive Grace*.

> Martyr, prophet, and statesman may each in his own way be servant of the Kingdom. Without the martyr we might live under the illusion that the kingdom of Caesar is the Kingdom of Christ in embryo and forget that there is a fundamental contradiction between the two kingdoms. Without the successful prophet, whose moral indictments effect actual changes in the world, we might forget that each moment of human history faces actual and realizable higher possibilities. Without the statesman, who uses power to correct the injustices of power, we might allow the vision of the Kingdom of Christ to become a luxury of those who can afford to acquiesce in present injustice because they do not suffer from it.[83]

In this passage, Niebuhr is not explicitly referring to the three offices of Christ, but they are clearly in the background of his message. This is precisely the type of multidimensional thinking for which I have been lobbying in this book. However, later generations may come to the conclusion that the deepest modern thinker with regard to the ethics of violence is not a defender of force such as Niebuhr, nor a pacifist such as Yoder, but that strange Danish author Kierkegaard. He may actually be the most subtle and far-seeing visionary, because he put his finger on the one thing needful: to become oneself before God by listening to the voice of Christ whose love for us loves forth our love for our neighbor (WL, 216–17).

I have argued that fundamentalism, individualism, and utopianism are all in agreement that evil must be overcome through evil. We are now at a point where we can see the alternative, which the apostle Paul articulated in his epistle to the Romans: "Do not be overcome by evil, but overcome evil with good" (Rom 12:21). This is a perfect summary of Christ's life and message. Those who argue in favor of pacifism are on the most solid ground here in terms of the interpretation of scripture. Christ's victory over evil, won on the Cross, was through the witness of nonviolent love. Activist leaders in our times such as Gandhi and Martin Luther King Jr. are walking in this same stream of witness. They understood and taught very clearly that genuine social transformation cannot come out of retaliation, but only out of a willingness to suffer within oneself the outpouring of violence. But the just use of force position, at its best, is also a refraction of the principle of overcoming evil

83. Niebuhr, *Reinhold Niebuhr on Politics*, 209.

with good. This position is admittedly paradoxical, in that it is willing to use measured force to stop a greater evil, but it also is rooted in the good. It does not stand idly by when the good of human life is threatened by demonic mayhem. It takes effective action to limit evil, drawing on the authority that God has built into creation by declaring his creatures good and their lives valuable and worthy of protection.[84]

I have been drawing here on the themes of Christ the Priest and Christ the King, but Christ the Prophet will have the last word:

> At that very time there were some present who told him about the Galileans whose blood Pilate had mingled with their sacrifices. He asked them, "Do you think that because these Galileans suffered in this way they were worse sinners than all other Galileans? No, I tell you; but unless you repent, you will all perish as they did. Or those eighteen who were killed when the tower of Siloam fell on them—do you think that they were worse offenders than all the others living in Jerusalem? No, I tell you; but *unless you repent*, you will all perish just as they did." (Luke 13:1–5, emphasis mine)

Evil is overcome "one by one from the inside out," as the saying goes. The ultimate solution to the problem of evil in human history is the growth of the self through conversion to God.[85] As long as we remain immature as human beings, always seeking to reinforce our immaturity, we will do evil and we will respond in kind when others do evil. The energy feeding into violence will only be drained away when we as human beings allow our spirits to be transformed by God, our Creator, who is always seeking to draw us forward into fullness of life as persons created in God's triune image. The message of Christ the Prophet accomplishes this spiritual transformation. We will overcome evil with good when we become good (mature, complex, expansive) by modeling ourselves after the Son, who modeled himself after the Father in the power of the Spirit.

84. Craig Carter argues that Christians have an either/or choice: either to be completely nonviolent or to use the sword to coerce others to profess the Christian faith (*Rethinking Christ and Culture*, 209). This is a false dichotomy.

85. See Kierkegaard, *Upbuilding Discourses in Various Spirits*, 122–54. These reflections on disentangling the self from the crowd prepare the ground for his ethical message in *Works of Love*.

PART THREE

Rhetoric

It is blasphemous to want to make God one's collaborator in hating.
—Søren Kierkegaard, *Works of Love*, 262

All oppressors and wrongdoers love to provoke violence so that their own suppressions and original violence will seem justified to themselves and to others.
—Sidney Cornelia Callahan, *With All Our Heart and Mind*, 135

Revenge mistakenly appears to be a soothing of one's pain, but in the light of truth it is seen to be only evil contending with evil. What difference is there between the one who provokes and the one provoked except that the one is caught doing wrong sooner than the other? Nevertheless, before the Lord each is guilty of having injured a fellow man and the Lord forbids and condemns every act of wrong-doing. There is no hierarchical arrangement in wrong-doing, nor does position make any distinction in that which similarity makes one. Therefore, the precept is unequivocally laid down: evil is not to be rendered for evil.
—Tertullian, *Disciplinary, Moral, and Ascetical Works*, 210

When private affections extend themselves to a considerable number, we are ready to look upon them as truly virtuous, and accordingly to applaud them highly. Thus it is with respect to a man's love to a large party, or a country . . . Hence, among the Romans, love to their country was the highest virtue; though this affection of theirs so much extolled, was employed as it were for the destruction of the rest of mankind.

—Jonathan Edwards, *The Nature of True Virtue*, 88

Since the self judges itself by its own standards it finds itself good. It judges others by its own standards and finds them evil, when their standards fail to conform to its own. This is the secret of the relationship between cruelty and self-righteousness.

—Reinhold Niebuhr, *The Nature and Destiny of Man*, I:199

It is only as self-critical that we have any right to consider ourselves recipients of divine revelation.

—James Alison, *Faith Beyond Resentment*, 159

. . . everything which is evil from Adam to our own day, from the great horrors of world history down to the little lies and acts of unfriendliness with which we have mutually poisoned our lives, springs from human hate of God's grace.

—Karl Barth, *God Here and Now*, 89

I cannot build my children's future on the hatreds of the past, nor can I teach them to love God more by loving people less.

—Jonathan Sacks, *The Dignity of Difference*, 190

6

Kierkegaard's Critique of the 9/11 Hijackers

Or, Does a Human Being Have the Right to Commit Suicide While Also Committing Mass Murder for His Idolatrous Notion of the Truth?

No. Now that we have answered the vexing question in our title, we can begin our ethical-religious essay.

The main question that spurs Kierkegaard to write his essay "Does a Human Being Have the Right to Let Himself Be Put to Death for the Truth?" concerns the apparent willingness of Christ to let human beings become guilty of the crime of killing him (WA, 51–89). Surely, if Christ were motivated by love, he would not have let this happen; he would have found some way of leading humanity away from this pit of defiled conscience into which they were determined to throw themselves through the wrongful exercise of their free will. Surely God, in compassion and concern for his creatures, could have found some way to soften the situation, to make it less severe.

But no, the severity remained in place because it is impossible that the Holy One who is the Truth could compromise in some way with the sinful world. A collision was inevitable, not because God the Father demanded the bloody sacrifice of his Son, but because the proclamation of the Truth about who God is and who we are could be accomplished in no other way. The Atonement of the human race, its reconciliation with God, is not an event that can happen through gentle persuasion and education, but only through a dramatic event that breaks apart reality as we know it. Things *must* happen this way not because violence has its starting point in God, but because we human beings have chosen the path of violence as an expression of our refusal to participate in the divine life. It is our intransigence, the ferocity with which we hold fast to our fallenness, that dictates that God must deal with us in a severe way.

There is, therefore, at the core of Christ's identity, a sense of mission that can only come to completion in martyrdom. He was the Truth; he was Love; and in this world truth and love are hated and rejected. He was the Witness, the Martyr. But he was also, as Kierkegaard said many times, the Prototype, the one who shows us what it is to be a human being. He calls us to follow in his footsteps. It makes sense, then, that believers would seek to imitate Christ so literally that they also become witnesses and martyrs by giving up their lives in service to the Truth. Did he not predict that this is precisely what would happen? "Blessed are those who are persecuted for righteousness' sake, for theirs is the kingdom of heaven. Blessed are you when people revile you and persecute you and utter all kinds of evil against you falsely on my account. Rejoice and be glad, for your reward is great in heaven, for in the same way they persecuted the prophets who were before you" (Matt 5:10–12).

In the wake of Christ, who was himself the Truth, and was put to death because he was the Truth, is there not a natural human desire to ally oneself with the cause of God by being a martyr also? Christ turned upside down the ancient notion that truth is on the side of the government or the crowd that is attacking and condemning the victim. René Girard's writings have established this point quite convincingly. Western history is the story of the dethronement of sacred societal violence by the Christ event as it is recounted in the gospels. The gospels have prevailed over human untruth by establishing that truth is on the side of the victim, not the mob. "The crowd is untruth," as Kierkegaard said so forcefully. Does it not make sense, then, that a person will desire to abide in the truth in a visible way by taking on the role of the martyr?

In the essay we are considering, however, ("Has a Man the Right") Kierkegaard is suspicious of this desire, because it contradicts one of the clearest commands of all: our duty to love the neighbor. If I play the role of the martyr I am allowing others to become guilty of my death. I am thus placing them in the position of condemnation and perdition so that I can fly away to enjoy the blessedness of heaven. "Does a *human being* have the right to go that far? Does he, even if he is in the right and has truth on his side, does he have the right to make others guilty in this way, does he have the right to bring such a punishment upon others" (WA, 69)? Is this not the epitome of selfishness? Can it really be the case that Christ came to earth simply to give a select few a more refined way of being egoistic? Surely not. Something is wrong with this picture. If Christ taught us anything, it is that we are to hold our fellow human beings in our love and concern. We are to be neighbors to them, never forgetting our equality before God with them because we are all children of the same Creator. We are to take responsibility for them; we are to obey the command to love them and accept the duties that follow from the command. To be concerned only for oneself and not for the well-being of others, and to act in such a way that those others will suffer a terrible judgment in the future, is actually a form of cruelty: "Most people have difficulty in seeing my issue. They say that it is cruel to put him, the innocent one, to death, but I ask: Was it not cruel of him or is it not cruel of him to others to let the matter come to the point where they did put or they do put him to death?" (WA, 72).

This is one side of the argument, which clearly works against approval of voluntary martyrdom. But what is the other side of the argument? Kierkegaard lays this out as well. The martyr(1) "remains faithful to himself and fulfills absolutely his duty to the truth", (2) has "an awakening effect and thus helps truth to be victorious", and (3) serves by his life and death as "an awakening example for later generations" (WA, 72). This strand of Christian faith has a long and distinguished history from St. Stephen and the apostles up to Martin Luther King Jr. and Oscar Romero in our own time. Why is it that despite understanding the logic of this position, and respecting the depth of faith that gives rise to it, Kierkegaard remains uncomfortable with it?

"Does a human being, even if he is in the right and has the truth on his side, have the right to let others makes themselves guilty of a murder? The question is: Can the solitary human being in relation to other human beings be assumed to be in absolute possession of the truth? If not, then an absolute duty to something of which I do not have absolute possession involves a contradiction" (WA, 73). Kierkegaard draws a distinction between Christ, who had an absolute possession of the truth because he was the Truth, and the rest of the human race. Christ's death is a retroactive atonement for the guilt incurred by those who caused his death, and an anticipatory atonement for future guilt as well. Christ's work takes into consideration *the race* and its spiritual situation on the broadest possible horizon. But you and I, as sinful, finite individuals are not Christ. Our work cannot be equated with his, lest we fall into absurd hubris. We may also fall into an absurd self-righteousness: "Do I, then, myself a human being who belongs to the evil world, dare to say that the world in relation to me is evil, is sinful, that is, that I am pure and holy" (WA, 76)? No, I dare not say that. If I see clearly, I will not build a wall between myself and others, using as bricks a belief that I am superior to them in some decisive way. I will not pretend to be God's soldier in distinction from other people that I have labeled as servants of evil.

The kinship of all human beings—our solidarity in error and finitude—prevents us from presuming that we have the right to let others put us to death for the truth. Kierkegaard arrives at this judgment with a notable remark: "this conclusion makes me very sad" (WA, 84). It is sad because the fullness with which we may wish to gesticulate our deepest convictions must be trimmed back. Instead of living in a world of intense light and intense darkness, we must be content to live in shades of gray. This conclusion will not satisfy those who are tempted to inhabit the extremes, but it is clearly the humane message that we need to hear in our day.

~

If we are looking for a contemporary perversion of what Kierkegaard's pseudonym Johannes de Silentio meant by the "teleological suspension of the ethical," it is hard to find a clearer example than the 9/11 terrorist attacks. The hijackers knew that what they were doing would be condemned by "ethics" as it is currently understood in Muslim, Christian, or philosophical terms, but they believed that these conceptions of ethics had no real power to constrain them, because they were obeying a divine mandate that transcended the normal categories in which people think. They understood themselves as living in obedience to the will of God, which trumps all other directives whenever there is a conflict between competing voices in the human mind.

Perhaps they were right. Perhaps they were truly obeying the will of God. That is all that can be said in their defense—perhaps. But the implications of their being in the right with regard to the character of God are so horrendous that this "obedience" on their part can only be an omen of a future for the human race that is utterly bleak. On the other hand, a great deal more can be said in criticism of their way of thinking and acting. We can produce an autopsy of their derailed form of spiritual existence that is quite detailed and extensive. I will merely touch on the highlights here.[1]

There are three main dimensions of reality as it is experienced by human beings: (1) *the vertical axis* (the relationship between the individual and God); (2) *the temporal trajectory* (the self's relationship with its past, present, and future); and (3) *the horizontal plane* (the human being's relationships with other human beings). Each of these dimensions can be either healthy or sick, on the right track or derailed.

Sickness on the vertical axis typically takes one of two forms, either conscious rebellion against God, or conscious fidelity to God that is actually masking an underlying idolatry. The first form is analyzed by Kierkegaard in that section of *The Sickness unto Death* in which he describes "defiance" as despairingly willing to be oneself over against God (SUD, 67–74). The second form, idolatry, is the other side of the coin, because it is also a form of defiance. Instead of simply rejecting God, the idolater chooses to relate to a god of his own invention that serves as an enabler of his deepest desires. By refusing to relate to the true God who is the Creator of the self, the idolater hollows out the image of God and fills in the hole with his own maniacal energy:

> The more consciousness there is in such a sufferer who in despair wills to be himself, the more his despair intensifies and becomes demonic. It usually originates as follows. A self that in despair wills to be itself is pained in some distress or other that does not allow itself to be taken away from or separated from his concrete self. So now he makes precisely this torment the object of all his passion, and finally it becomes a demonic rage. By now, even if God in heaven and all the angels offered to help him out of it—no, he does not want that, now it is too late. Once he would gladly have given everything to be rid of this agony, but he was kept waiting; now it is too late, now he would rather rage against everything and be the wronged victim of the whole world and of all life, and it is of particular significance to him to make sure that he has his torment on hand and that no one takes it away from him—for then he would not be able to demonstrate and prove to himself that he is right. This eventually becomes such a fixation that for an extremely strange reason he is afraid of eternity, afraid that it will separate him from his, demonically understood, infinite superiority over other men,

1. For further reading, see Cooper, *New Political Religions*.

> his justification, demonically understood, for being what he is. (SUD, 72)

If modern history has taught us anything, it is that the human beings who have the strongest sense of their own victimhood are the ones who are most likely to be ferociously violent. This was the case with the Nazis, and it is clearly the case today with those Muslim extremists who are fixated on the glory of the Islamic past and what they perceive as the victimization of Muslims today by the United States and Israel. That there has been such victimization in reality is well-nigh impossible to disentangle from the psychological fantasies and demonic behaviors to which it gives rise. The salient point for our purposes here is the notion that when a person enters the mode of generating an image of God out of his own frustrations with himself and his historical context, the theological content of that image will typically be a god who demands a sacrifice. Blood must be spilled to restore the lost balance of the cosmos.

At the root of idolatry is a refusal to grow up into the human being that God wants one to become. "Not willing to be oneself before God" is the key concept in *The Sickness unto Death*; it signifies a stunted selfhood that insists upon remaining stunted. In other words, there is a kind of idolization of oneself that precedes the idolization of God. By affirming oneself as the ultimate judge of oneself and controller of reality, one is usurping the place of God and must invent a new god out of one's imagination. But this type of spiritually derailed self-assertion means that the person is rejecting the deeper, truer self that God is calling into being in each moment. In Kierkegaard's words: "the most insane pride is the pride that oscillates between idolizing and despising oneself" (WA, 61). What is being idolized is the stunted self and what is being despised is the growing-toward-maturity self. In other words, the second dimension of reality, which is constituted by the self's existence within the trajectory of time, has become disturbed. The self chooses not to live in the fullness of time, which involves accepting the divine source of one's being (the past) and responding to the call of creation (the future). The self is left only with itself, hemmed in by its frantic attempt to fortify itself in the present moment.

What we call "fundamentalism" is a product of this state of spiritual disturbance, which generates an idol by inventing an arbitrary and violent image of God. This idolization process insists that this god is the source of reality, the Creator, whose will was revealed in a Golden Age in the past—an age that becomes another idol to which sacrifices must be made. Thus the stunted self is trapped in a very narrow present that tricks itself into believing that it speaks for the past. In reality, the immature self is incapable of truly learning from the past; it cannot fathom the idea that the wisdom of past (and the sacred scriptures it gave us) is a living force that seeks to enter into us and transform us into the growing-toward-maturity persons that we ought to be.

The third main dimension of reality is the horizontal plane—relationship with the neighbor. It is a basic axiom of Kierkegaard's anthropology that when the first two dimensions of reality—relationship with God and with self—are disturbed, there will be negative ramifications in the sphere of sociality. This journal passage expresses the link clearly: "Love to God and love to neighbor are like two doors that open simultaneously, so that it is impossible to open the one without opening the other, and impossible to shut one without also shutting the other" (JP, 3:2434). This statement summarizes the teachings of Jesus and the New Testament as a whole. "God is love" and "he who hates his brother is in the darkness" are the paired assertions from John 1 that form the heart of Kierkegaard's message in *Works of Love*. For our purposes here in this essay, it is important to emphasize that just as the idolization of God begins within the sickness of the stunted self, so also does misrelation with the neighbor. Because the immature self seeks to fight off the possibility of giving up its arrogant desire to control reality for its own protection, it requires an enemy that it can turn into an object to attack. What is actually happening at a deeper level is the self's attack on its better self; but in the twisted and confused world of the stunted self, the attack is thought to be against an external enemy, not an internal one. Other human beings must be turned into scapegoats who are killed as part of the self's efforts in self-preservation. When a society is made up of stunted selves, as societies usually are, then there will be a meeting of minds in a common purpose. In order to protect ourselves from the possibility of growing, the unconscious logic states, we must band together against the Other, the outsider, the evil one, the Great Satan. Our triumph over our enemy will ensure the protection of our way of life. What is the way of life that is being protected? There are stock answers to this question that arise out of the derailed mind, but the real answer is that the way of life that is being protected is idolatry, stunted selfhood, and the continual justification of acts of violence against others.

The perfect synthesis of this way of life was seen in the 9/11 attacks. The attacks were justified in the minds of the hijackers because of their idolatrous belief that they were obeying the will of God. The other human beings who were attacked and killed were mostly civilians going about their jobs. In other words, they were the Neighbor, the fellow human being whom we are all called by God to love and protect. The act of suicide is the ultimate expression of the violence that arises out of stunted selfhood, because it reveals the true motive of the violence. The self wants to kill itself to avoid the pain and anxiety involved in the event of coming into existence as a human being before God. The most effective way to fend off the possibility of willing to be oneself before God is to kill the self. This is not martyrdom arising out of genuine faith, but simply suicide arising out of cowardice in the face of the demands of existing as a spiritual being in this world before God and with the neighbor. Christ's "free decision to will to die is in eternal agreement with the Father's will. When a human being wills his death, this is tempting God, because no human being dares to presume such an agreement with God" (WA, 65).

At the beginning of this essay, I answered "No" to the title's question. I have now made the reasoning underlying that judgment as clear as I know how to make it.

To draw this essay to a close, we will consider the broad outline of Kierkegaard's vision of the human pathway into the life of God.

Sin entails alienation from God, resistance to growth in selfhood, and enmity toward other human beings. The last aspect needs to be nuanced with the observation that there may be "preferential love" shown toward certain other people that contrasts with the enmity toward the "enemy." But in *Works of Love*, Kierkegaard points out that this preferential, worldly love can turn into its opposite, hate (WL, 34). It is an unstable and illusory form of love in contrast with the abiding love that is a gift from above. Preferential love forms alliances, crowds, gangs, and mobs. The first step towards salvation is thus a dual movement: (1) the disentangling of the self from the crowd (which has as its animating spirit alienation from God), and (2) the opening up of the self to its true destiny through loving God. My listing of these as (1) and (2) should not be interpreted as a temporal order, as if we could know whether the chicken or the egg comes first. The essential movement is a transfer of allegiance, away from one's social milieu as a counterfeit god and maker of souls, to the true Creator of heaven and earth. Kierkegaard emphasizes again and again throughout his authorship that God is the central point around which reality pivots.

When God's Spirit opens up our spirits, the love and grace of God enter into us and change us from within. God recreates us in God's image, which means that our character will be shaped by God's peacefulness, beauty, and love. No longer will we be characters in a drama written by the world. We will be characters in God's play, taking our cues from our new Prototype, Christ. Instead of learning from "the others" whom we should hate, we will learn from Christ that we are freed to love all people as our neighbor. The grammar is actually turned around, as we learn from him that we should not be anxious about determining who exactly our neighbor is; rather, *we are commanded to be the neighbor* to all we encounter on our earthly walk (WL, 22). To love the neighbor and to be the neighbor are two sides of the same coin. It is just as accurate to say that loving the neighbor and loving the self are two sides of the same coin. And those two loves are the fruit of our love for God, which is the fruit of God's "loving forth love" in us (WL, 217). "If you want to show that your life is intended to serve God, then let it serve people, yet continually with the thought of God" (WL, 161).

These movements that we have been tracing map out the topography of grace, which is another way of saying Trinity. The Father loves the Son and gives him to the world in the power of the Spirit; the Spirit enables us to respond with openness to the Creator and the event of creation. In this event, we move toward the fullness of what it means to be a human being that Christ demonstrated for us. When we love the neighbor in response to the gracious and freeing command of God, we are living as co-creators along with the Father, the Son, and the Spirit. "Just as Christianity's joyful message is contained in the doctrine of humanity's inherent kinship with God, so is Christianity's task humanity's likeness to God. But God is love, and therefore we can be like God only in loving, just as we also, according to the words of the apostle, can only be *God's co-workers—in love*" (WL, 62–63).

The Holy Spirit is referred to in the New Testament as the Paraclete, a Greek term that means "the counsel for the defense," as contrasted with Satan, who is the prosecuting attorney, the Accuser. When we live with and for God, we are led by the Holy Spirit to take up the cause of our fellow human beings, to come to their defense, even and especially when they are filled with the world's rancor. This is how we can put our finger on the deepest and most essential difference between the world's false Jihad and the true Jihad to which God calls us. (I'm using the term "false Jihad" as a synonym for a "holy war" that could be engaged in by a member of any cultural or religious group.) The false Jihad tells us that we must attack other human beings after accusing them of wrongdoing (while remaining blind to our own wrongdoing). Saul of Tarsus was engaged in such a Jihad when we was approving of the stoning of Stephen. The 9/11 hijackers were engaged in such a false Jihad.

The world-transforming voice of truth that is the Holy Spirit teaches us that the true Jihad is not a struggle *against* flesh and blood but a struggle *for* flesh and blood. In other words, when we see in our fellow human beings the watermark that is God's image (WL, 89), we will love them as God loves them and seek to free them from their violence. We will be their advocate and defender, not the self-righteous agent of their condemnation and destruction. We return to the text that inspired our initial reflections in this essay:

> The untruth consists in this, that the one struggling in this way relates himself to the others only polemically, thinking only of himself, not lovingly considering their cause. But in that case he is very far from being truly superior to them or superior in truth, because superiority is to be the counsel for the defense of one's enemy and as such to be concerned and, with more insight than he has, to keep watch so that he does not falsely become more guilty than he deserves. (WA, 88)

Kierkegaard's suspicions regarding a simplistic affirmation of martyrdom are perfectly expressed here. The martyr, truly understood, is not the one who dies to condemn, but the one who dies to free others from condemnation. Christ is the martyr in this sense. But *our* calling is to remain in the land of the living, loving our fellow human beings and "loving forth love" in them so that they may be freed from living out the script of violence that has been written by Satan, not God.

The three main components of the theological method at work in this essay are theology, psychology, and ethics. This essay has covered those topics in reverse order. We began with Kierkegaard's "No" to voluntary martyrdom, which is rooted in his understanding of the ethical imperative to love the neighbor and maintain the bonds of human kinship. We then demonstrated how Kierkegaard's psychology allows us to understand the roots of violence. We concluded with reflections on the way of the human soul into the life of the triune God as the ultimate solution to the problem of violence in human history.

These three aspects of reality—who God is, who we are, and what we ought to do—are linked together with unbreakable bonds. This means that we cannot separate any of these three aspects from the others without waging war against reality. If we try to define ourselves as human beings without connection to God and to ethics, we end up with the insanity of Nietzsche. If we try to create an "ethical" society by rejecting God and denying the sanctity of each human life, we end up with the insanity of Stalinism. If we try to cleave to God while rejecting our selfhood and hating our neighbor, we end up with the insanity of the 9/11 hijackers.

Once we grasp the nature of these unbreakable bonds between the dimensions of reality, then we have no choice but to conclude that "the end justifies the means" thinking is a philosophical error that arises out of human psychopathology. There is no other end that trumps the ethical by being "higher." The ethical is intrinsically and eternally linked with authentic selfhood and God's work of continuing creation.

7

A Speech Not Given on September 20, 2001

Address to a Joint Session of Congress and the American People

Mr. Speaker, Mr. President Pro Tempore, members of Congress, and fellow Americans:

We have been struck by lightning. A small number of our fellow human beings have decided to place their own humanity in question by committing suicide in a way that intentionally included mass murder. We are shocked; we are stunned; we are in tremendous pain, as is the whole civilized world. After a century that witnessed the inhumanity of human beings to each other on an unprecedented scale, we are forced to begin this new century with yet another episode of bloody barbarity, as if we needed to be reminded of the depths of spiritual corruption to which human beings can descend.

When I say that we have been struck by lightning, I am using a term that I have chosen carefully. The history of the human race has demonstrated that even though most human beings most of the time are peace-loving and responsible citizens, it sometimes happens that particular individuals or groups choose to allow themselves to become lightning rods for evil. They become conduits for the entry into the world of heinous behaviors that cause tremendous pain and suffering. Adolf Hitler was such a lightning rod, along with Stalin and Pol Pot. Jim Jones and Timothy McVeigh were conduits of destruction. The members of the Ku Klux Klan showed themselves to be lightning rods for evil whenever they lynched a black person. I could continue this list until it is quite lengthy, but I will stop there. The point I am emphasizing is that even though we human beings are created in the image of God, we have the capacity to reject that image and become servants of an evil whose only goal seems to be the destruction of human life.

We are still learning about those who attacked us without warning and without making any demands, after they had apparently decided that the intentional slaughter of thousands of people was an action of which their conscience could approve. They were members of al Qaeda, a terrorist organization led by Osama bin Laden that has already killed many people in many different countries around the world. This group presents itself as the true voice of Islam. It is not. Islam, like all of the major religions of the world, is a religion of peace. The teachings of Islam specifically condemn suicide and the intentional murder of civilians. Osama bin Laden and his followers do not legitimately speak for the religion of Islam, just as the KKK does not speak legitimately for Christianity. In each case, a group of psychologically deranged people is seeking to hijack a religion, in defiance of the well established ethical traditions of humanity, to turn that religion into a weapon for the wanton destruction of human life.

In America, Muslims practice their religion alongside Christians, Jews, Buddhists, and Hindus. Such freedom of religion is a model that other countries around the world would do well to emulate. American Muslims are appalled by the actions of a small number of extremists who claim to be acting on behalf of Allah, when they are actually blaspheming Allah and doing immense damage to Islam as a religion. American Muslims realize that it may take decades or even centuries to repair the damage that has been done to the public image of Islam. I want to assure all Muslims who are listening to my words that I respect your faith; I fully realize that the struggle we face in the future is a struggle not against Islam as a religion, but against those people who attack the Muslim faith by turning it into a projection of their own twisted egos, because their love of death and killing is greater than their love for anything else.

There are those who say that in the past the human race was religious, but in the modern period the human race is becoming secularized, and religion will gradually wither away. I do not support this view. On the contrary, I believe that the twenty first century will be intensely religious and theological. I say this because we have arrived at a historic crossroads in our journey as a race. Two paths have opened up before us that lead in very different directions. These paths are theological. Along one path, God is viewed as having a mean streak, a violent side. This God is wrathful and he demands sacrifices; he is a God of vengeance who expects his faithful followers to purify the world through acts of violence against those who have been labeled by those followers as the enemies of God. The worshippers of this God believe that they understand his will perfectly and are commissioned to carry it out, leaving a bloody trail in their wake. Along the other path, God is understood to be the champion of justice who seeks to protect all people from unjust attacks. This God is loving, compassionate, and gracious. This God does not continually demand sacrifices and rejoice in the spilling of blood. On the contrary, he is distressed by the violent actions of his children, who so often stray from the true path that leads to joy and life. The followers of this God do not assume that they have a perfect knowledge of his will, since this God transcends the limits of human understanding. They seek to increase in their knowledge of this God by studying the sacred scriptures and allowing the texts to point them in the direction of peace and reconciliation, with justice. It is my belief that these two very different visions of God will constitute the central question being debated within the human race in the twenty first century. Which one is our Creator? Which one is worthy of our praise and obedience?

Another key set of questions that will be asked in the twenty first century are those that center around the problem of understanding ourselves as human beings. Why are we violent? What motivates us to think and act the way we do? What are our potentials for change and transformation? These are vitally important questions, and we need not throw up our hands in despair of ever answering them. In fact, our leading thinkers, from previous centuries and today, have reflected deeply on these questions and have made significant strides toward answering them. Unfortunately, the insights of these thinkers have not become the common knowledge of the human race in general. There is a gap between the wisdom that our religious and philosophical teachers are able to offer us, and the lack of understanding that marks our citizenry. This situation is reminiscent of earlier centuries when certain key scientists began to understand the movements of the stars and planets more clearly than they had been understood in the past. It took a period of centuries before the insights of the cutting edge scientists, such as Copernicus, worked their way down into the basic levels of the educational system in the Western world. I hope that it won't take quite that long for the knowledge gained by religious leaders and social scientists to work its way into our educational system so that the children of future generations can grow up understanding human behavior competently.

All of the major religious traditions of humanity have strong ethical teachings that prohibit intentional murder. When religious leaders denounce acts of violence committed by terrorists, they are drawing on these traditions. But more is needed than denunciation. Our religious leaders and our educators at all levels of study need to apply themselves diligently to the task of developing a deep understanding of how the human psyche becomes derailed, leading to unethical behavior. They need to be able to unveil, through a well articulated vision of the shape of the healthy human soul, the falseness of an ideology that seeks to justify turning human beings into expendable objects. Our cultural leaders need to have something other than just a different opinion than those who commit terrorist acts; they need to have a significantly superior insight into human psychology. Developing this insight is the task that lies before them in the coming decades. I hope that these words convey a message that is loud and clear to the intellectual leaders of the Christian, Jewish, and Muslim communities.

There are those who are saying today that the attacks we have suffered prove that "religion causes violence." This is a tired phrase that ought to be abandoned because it lacks philosophical coherence. "Religion" is an abstract concept that is very difficult to define, even for those who specialize in its study. It is not an active agent that makes people do things. There is no puppet-master called "religion" that has the power to override the free will of human beings. To suggest that there is is to put the cart before the horse. Those human beings who carry out violent acts do so for reasons that arise out of their psychopathology. If they have confused and contradictory religious ideas in their heads, and use religious rhetoric to support their hypocritical actions, this is a byproduct of their derangement, not its cause. History has shown us very clearly that atheists can be just as violent as those who are ostensibly religious; and agnostics can be just as active in working for peace as believers. So the tired phrase "religion causes violence" clearly shows that the person uttering it finds reality a bit too difficult to comprehend, leading them to give up on the task too soon.

We have been attacked. We must now reflect on how we will respond to what has happened to us—what has happened to the world. Firstly, we need to grieve with those families whose loved ones have been murdered. The grieving process is not simple and it is not quick. Those whose lives were taken will leave behind a huge hole in the hearts of their family members and friends—a hole that will contain immense pain for years to come. We must reach out to those who are mourning to support them in every way possible. We are all grieving as a nation, and we will be for years. Let us remember those who are no longer with us and receive from them a mission to carry on in our own lives all that they taught us about friendship, love, laughter, faith, and human decency. As we do so, we will honor their memory in the most fitting and upbuilding way, and we will live through and in our grief as survivors who are made stronger, not weaker, by suffering.

In the days following last Tuesday, people from all around the globe have been grieving along with us. On behalf of the American people, I thank you for your sympathy, your prayers, and your support. Prayers have been said for us in dozens of different languages, in England, Poland, Egypt, Australia, South Africa, Brazil, South Korea, India, and many other countries. Our national anthem has been played at Buckingham Palace, on the streets of Paris, and at Berlin's Brandenburg Gate. The whole civilized world has understood that this has been an attack not just on the United States, but on humanity itself. Along with thousands of Americans, citizens of 80 other nations were killed in the attacks. As the world grieves with us, we will use this opportunity to strengthen our ties with other nations, to build a strong coalition that will be able to undermine effectively the threat of terrorism in the coming years.

We must also use these dark and painful days as an opportunity for deep and sustained reflection on the shortcomings of all human beings, ourselves included. This is never a comforting message to hear. We naturally want to think well of ourselves and to compare ourselves favorably to others. It makes us feel good to see ourselves as being in the right, as being on the side of God, as being defenders of freedom against despots and their minions. Conversely, we have a natural desire to identify a selected group of other human beings as our enemies, who have a character that is diametrically opposed to ours. "They are evildoers;

they hate freedom and goodness and morality; they are the children of Satan." This is the way we are tempted to describe them. If we allow the attacks that we have suffered to draw us into this way of thinking about ourselves and about those Others, then we have allowed the terrorists to dictate how we think and feel by making us their clones. That is what we must not do. This way of thinking that simplistically divides the world into two camps is a kind of sickness; it falsifies reality rather than clarifying it. In truth, all human beings are fallible. We are all capable of good and of evil. All cultural groups and nations have positive aspects and unfortunate flaws. Serious reflection on our own flaws, mistakes, and selfish actions is the pathway we must follow if we wish to lead humanity in a better direction in the future. It should not require an act of heinous violence to bring us to this realization. To take stock of our failings as individuals and as nations should be our continual practice.

Throughout the whole civilized world, there is an institution within society that is charged with the task of tracking down and apprehending those persons who have shown themselves to be at war with the Law by committing intentional acts of violence. The police do this difficult and dangerous job day in and day out. The attacks that we have suffered have reminded us forcefully just how courageous, dedicated, and selfless these public servants are. They risk their lives for us, to keep us as safe as we can be kept in this unpredictable world. Many of them lost their lives last Tuesday, rushing into burning buildings to help others get out of them. We will continue the work that they did to honor their memory. We will use all of the resources available to us, including our armed forces if necessary, to track down and bring to justice those who are directly responsible for planning these attacks. We will work with the international community to apprehend and bring to justice those who are indirectly responsible for the attacks by providing safe haven and encouragement to the terrorists. We will do this to protect human life from those who do not value either their own lives or the lives of others.

There may be some persons who will say that our response to the attacks we have suffered should be an expression of our *revenge* on the "evildoers." Revenge is a deeply human emotion. It arises out of a desire to honor the dead and act in their place because they can no longer act for themselves. But it is an emotion whose place in human life belongs to the past, not to the future. Revenge seeks to balance the scales of justice by adding more killings to those that have already occurred. This is not the sort of balance that we should be seeking. What we need is not a balancing of the scales, but a transformation of human culture, such that we learn new ways of relating to each other.

There are those who will say in the coming months and years that these attacks we have suffered are a sign of things to come. We will be told that the terrorists will continue to attack us and they will use more and more lethal weapons. Therefore we must attack them first. We must forge a policy, in other words, that arises out of a politics of fear. We must listen to the voice of our own fears, and whip up the fears of the public so that they will support our newly devised plans to attack our enemies with ferocity. We must not only punish those who have already committed crimes, but we must clairvoyantly predict who is going to commit a crime in the future so that we can kill or capture them before they have a chance to do so. I do not agree with this view and I will not go down that path. This does not mean that I am naïve and do not have an understanding of how dangerous the world is; it means that the politics of fear is a self-fulfilling prophecy. By seeking to kill the terrorists we will only create more and more terrorists. We will be drawn down into a vortex of violence that has no end. No. We will not go down that path.

We do not have a crystal ball. We cannot see the future with certainty to know what is going to happen. We can live in the present with the clearest possible understanding of the past and with a vision of the future that traces a trajectory of ethical development for the human race. As Martin Luther King Jr. once said, "I do not know what the future holds, but I know who holds the future." We cannot manage and control history to make it come out according to our wishes, but we can live with courage and hope, knowing that the fabric of the universe, as it has been established by the Creator, tends toward justice and toward peace. Those who, through their actions, place themselves at war with the human race and its Creator are fighting against the grain of the universe. They will come unraveled one day, with or without any assistance from us, because they are actively refusing to be a part of the fabric that the Creator is making.

When attacked by evil, we are tempted to respond in kind. But one of the great religious teachers of human history, the apostle Paul, said: "Do not be overcome by evil, but overcome evil with good." These words are profoundly meaningful today. They present us with a question and a challenge. What does it mean to overcome evil with good? How does one do that? They challenge us to be the kind of people who can ask such a question seriously, seek answers to it creatively, and live out those answers with courage and hope. Underlying Paul's words is the insight that, in many circumstances, suffering must simply be endured. We cannot avoid suffering by inflicting suffering on others after we have suffered loss. Inflicting pain on others will not cancel our pain. The insight that Paul is expressing here arises directly out of the life and death of the man known to history as Jesus, son of Joseph and Mary. This lowly carpenter from a backwater town in a remote province of the Roman Empire two thousand years ago gave us the clearest model we have for overcoming evil with good. The Western world, with its long heritage of looking to this man for guidance, is a sphere where his teachings and example have a fighting chance of being heard and responded to. I hope and pray that we are up to that challenge.

In the Muslim community, the names of the prophets Noah, Abraham, Moses, Jesus, and Mohammed are pronounced with great respect, accompanied by the phrase, "peace be upon him." While verses in the Qur'an and the Bible can always be twisted out of context to support violent acts today, the heart of the message of the Qur'an and the Bible is a vision of peace and harmony within the human community. In the century that lies before us, a tremendous opportunity has opened up for respectful dialogue between the members of the main religions of Western civilization: Judaism, Christianity, and Islam. Out of that dialogue will grow a new world in which arguments in favor of mayhem and destruction will have no place, other than on the ash heap of discarded ideologies. The leaders of these three great religions need to develop a common message that can be communicated to those contemplating suicidal violence, a word such as this: "The whole human race needs you to stay with us in the land of the living. If you believe that by killing yourself and others you are making the world better, you are mistaken. If you truly have a desire to make the world better and struggle against evil, remain alive, and pour all of your energies into finding ways to improve the world through nonviolent means."

Americans have a long tradition of seeing themselves as "a city set on a hill," giving light to the nations. This will only be the case if our lives are characterized by the virtues of faith, hope, and love. The opposites of these are rebellion against God, suicidal despair, and hatred of one's fellow human beings. These vices were abundantly displayed by those who attacked us. The key to overcoming evil with good is not allowing the vicious to shape and determine our actions by drawing us into a vortex in which we mimic their violence.

By long standing tradition, it is customary for a speech such as this to end with a plea for God to bless the United States. We do make that plea today, with as much depth of feeling as we ever have in our nation's history. But we also pray for God to bless all of the nations of the world, not just our own, and we ask the Lord our Creator to give all human beings the wisdom that we will require to navigate humanely the very difficult years and decades that lie ahead of us.

Coda

As I was writing this speech, I was wrestling with the issue of plausibility. I had to express ideas that are at least remotely plausible as things that George W. Bush could say. Yet I also had to communicate ideas that are in my head and not in his head. Herein lies the difficulty. He and I are both human beings. We share a common humanity and a common Christian faith that build a bridge between us. Yet our varied life experiences, talents, relationships, and education have made us different people. (You as the reader of this book are in the same situation in relation to me as the author of this book and to George Bush; we are all different, yet we all share a common humanity.) This means that the speech I have written is both plausible and implausible at the same time. In other words, plausibility is clearly not suitable as a category within which the speech can be judged. What is the correct category? I will leave that with you as a question to ponder.

Instead of taking advantage of the golden opportunity that was made possible by horrific and tragic events, President Bush has responded with actions that are more predictable than they are creative and transformative. Terrorism is a *psychological* problem in the sense that there are people in our world whose thoughts and emotions are derailed in a way that leads them to commit deadly acts against average citizens in the hope of achieving political goals. But the primary response of the Bush administration is to seek a *military* solution to a *psychological* problem. The category mistake that is made in this way makes the problem worse because the military actions inflame the psychological derangement and spread it contagiously to more and more people.[1] The theory is that a plan of *limited* warfare and destruction can remedy the situation. This is the most accurate way to understand the naïve expectations of the Bush administration regarding how easy it would be to invade Iraq and establish democracy there. Eric Voegelin points us in the direction of an appropriate parallel drawn from history: Luther's belief that a *limited* destruction of the Catholic Church could fix the problems he was confronted with. Reflection on the violent aftermath of the Reformation informs us concerning "the situation of the man who wants to solve complicated social and intellectual problems through limited destruction" (CWEV, 22: 239). Voegelin's thought also emphasizes the insight that democracy cannot be magically imposed on a society from the top down. Rather, democracy only arises out of a healthy philosophy animating a coherent culture. Real democracy is the fruit of healthy human souls working together for the common good. Such conditions cannot be created by military action.

Jesus turned water into wine, he healed the sick, he fed the multitudes, he walked on water, he brought the dead back to life. It is perfectly obvious what he was: a sorcerer. He was not just *a* sorcerer, he was *The* Sorcerer. In comparison with him, Christians for the past two thousand years have been the Sorcerer's Apprentice. (Where is Reinhold Niebuhr when we need him to write an essay under that title?) We have been lazy and incompetent. We think that because we have been hanging around Jesus that we can do what he did. We think that we can tackle the problem of evil by ourselves, through our military adventures. But we do not know what we are doing and we make the situation worse rather than better. President Bush has been lazy by assigning the armed forces to be his broomstick by "winning the war on terror," when it is actually his job to fight that war through intellectual and spiritual power. In the wake of the 9/11 attacks, it was his task to make the common humanity of all human beings a reality rather than just a theory. If he had done so, he would have shown that he had actually learned something from Jesus. In Jesus, the common humanity of all human beings is a lived reality. Jesus reveals that to be human is to celebrate life and not to fear death, to walk in grace rather than in self-assertion or self-loathing, to love and

1. Jessica Stern concludes her study of terrorism with the observation that it is "a kind of virus." See *Terror in the Name of God*, 283.

not hate the neighbor. One who insists on labeling people as "evildoers" in preparation for killing them has failed to learn from Jesus.

The 9/11 hijackers understood themselves to be faithful to God. But they believed that there is no Us, no human solidarity, except in death, a point they apparently thought needed emphasizing. For them, there is no value to existence as a self in this world and there is no call to love the neighbor. There is only the imperative to present oneself before the judgment seat of God. And they apparently thought that God would be pleased to be presented with a cohort of mass-murderers. On what basis can we say that they were mistaken, that this God they were serving is an idol? We can say this because Jesus (peace be upon him) taught humanity that worship of God and murder of one's fellow human beings are mutually exclusive. This truth is equally accessible to Christians and Muslims, and it stands in judgment of both whenever they deny it.

8

Hypocrisy Is the Human Condition

Then David's anger was greatly kindled against the man. He said to Nathan, "As the Lord lives, the man who has done this deserves to die; he shall restore the lamb fourfold, because he did this thing, and because he had no pity." Nathan said to David, "You are the man!"

—II Sam. 12:5–7

"Let anyone among you who is without sin be the first to throw a stone at her." . . . When they heard it, they went away, one by one, beginning with the elders.

—John 8:7–9

THERE ARE PEOPLE WHO SAY, "I DON'T GO TO CHURCH BECAUSE IT'S full of hypocrites." While this observation about churchgoers is true, there are two problems with it. First, the statement seems to presume that the person making it is *not* a hypocrite. But this would indicate a self-righteous attitude that is at the heart of hypocrisy. The other small problem with the statement is that if our vision is clear, then we will realize that the world outside the church is also full of hypocrites. So as a reason for not going to church this line falls flat. I need to explain what I mean.

People in the modern world subscribe to many different philosophies and religious views. If we speak with persons who represent this variety and ask them if they are *evildoers*, would they say yes? Of course not. Everyone does what it is right in their own eyes. All actions *intend* a good (Aristotle). Those who are the most violent are often those who have the most highly developed sense of their own virtue. This statement is true across the spectrum from right to left. We are faced with the bald reality that human history is filled with people who are doing evil when they think they are doing good. The gap opened up here between rhetoric and reality is spanned by the word hypocrisy.

Hypocrisy is often defined in dictionaries as "pretending to be more religious or moral than you really are." While this is certainly accurate as a definition of how the word is often used, I would like to suggest a related definition that brings out the relational and judgmental aspect of the word, rather than just its mask-donning aspect. Hypocrisy can be defined as *accusing others of doing something wrong when you are also doing something wrong*. Note that this definition is intentionally vague; it does not say that hypocrisy is accusing others of doing something wrong when you yourself are doing *the same thing* wrong. That narrower definition, stated so forcefully by the apostle Paul, is certainly included within my broader definition. "Therefore you have no excuse, whoever you are, when you judge others; for in passing judgment on another you condemn yourself, because you, the judge, are doing the very same things" (Rom 2:1). But the broader definition takes into account the idea that we may accuse others of committing a certain sin that we are not guilty of; but we *are* guilty of other sins.

If the traditional theological idea that all people are sinners is true, and I believe it is, then we must come to an uncomfortable conclusion. According to the proposed definition of hypocrisy, it is an attitude that cannot be avoided, because we all do things wrong. In other words, hypocrisy is not a particular sin that could be placed in a list of sins such as greed, cruelty, lying, and so forth. Rather, hypocrisy is simply *the human condition. Hypocrisy is unavoidable because our interactions with other human beings will lead us to express disapproval of some of the things they are doing, and we are all sinners.*

How can this uncomfortable insight be escaped from? One possibility is to be sinless. In that case, one could accuse others of doing things wrong without doing anything wrong oneself. This may or may not be a logical possibility, but it is certainly not a realistic one. This is not reported in the Bible, but when Jesus said, "Let anyone among you who is without sin be the first to throw a stone," a rock flew through the air. He turned angrily toward a woman in the crowd and said, "Mother!" Philosophers tell us that the root of humor is incongruity, and the incongruity in this joke is clearly found in the idea that being holy would somehow lead a person to want to do violence to others with a perfect sense of their own moral superiority. Most of us are clear enough in our thinking to realize that it would be completely absurd for us to pretend that we never do anything wrong. For some of us, our consciousness is shaped by a weekly liturgy that reminds us of our sins of "thought, word, and deed," "what we have done and what we have left undone." Those whose consciousness is not shaped by words such as these nevertheless realize that they sometimes err in ways that harm others and damage relationships.

The second idea that comes to mind (as a possible escape from the uncomfortable conclusion) runs along these lines: "I don't want to be a hypocrite. Therefore I have decided not to judge anyone, for any reason. That is how I fend off your idea that hypocrisy is the human condition." This also strikes me as completely unrealistic, though I admit that its relative popularity as a way of thinking among "advanced" industrialized societies at least demonstrates that it has a certain plausibility to those who affirm it as a philosophy of life. The flaw in this concept is easy to see. If a man were beating his wife habitually and we were to say: "I don't judge wife-beating. That's okay. Whatever. It's a free country." Or, if a minority group were being oppressed by the majority in a country and we were to say: "I don't judge oppression. That's okay. Whatever." This sort of attitude, of course, is reprehensible for its apathy toward abuse and injustice. Wrongdoing *ought* to be judged. If we are thinking realistically, we will realize that judging is not only unavoidable but also commendable because when human beings are doing harm their actions ought to be disapproved of. In other words, the only way that we could completely avoid judging others is to be in a coma. The truth of this statement is seen in the observation that the person who says "I don't judge others because judging is wrong" is typically the most passionate critic of political leaders with whom he or she disagrees.

The comments that I have made regarding hypocrisy have been fairly abstract and formal, but their source is not simply logic. They arise out of my observations of myself and my fellow human beings. G. K. Chesterton cleverly observed that the doctrine of original sin is the one Christian doctrine that is empirically verifiable: "Certain new theologians dispute original sin, which is the only part of Christian theology which can really be proved."[1] Along similar lines, I maintain that the

1. Chesterton, *Orthodoxy*, first page of second chapter.

idea that hypocrisy is the human condition is obvious to anyone who has eyes to see. Let us consider some historical examples.

Think of the Israeli-Palestinian conflict. The Palestinians accuse the Israelis of being violent oppressors. The Israelis accuse the Palestinians of being violent terrorists. The most salient feature of this situation is that it is interminable because there is an element of truth in both accusations. Each side is (rightly) accusing the other of wrongdoing, while it is guilty of wrongdoing itself. For his book, *Terror in the Mind of God*, Mark Juergensmeyer interviewed activists on both sides of the conflict. He noted the remarkable similarity of vision and rhetoric used by both sides. Within each community, those who supported violent acts such as suicide bombings or machine gun attacks saw themselves as *victims*. The violence they approved of was always seen as *defensive*, even if it involved killing unarmed people who were praying at a place of worship or killing schoolchildren on a bus. Palestinian leader Dr. Abdul Rantisi put it this way:

> "We want to do the same to Israel as they have done to us," he explained, indicating that just as innocent Muslims had been killed in the Hebron incident and in many other skirmishes during the Israeli-Palestinian tensions, it was necessary for the Israeli people to actually experience the violence before they could understand what the Palestinians had gone through . . . "You think we are the aggressors," Rantisi said. "That is the number one misunderstanding. We are not: we are the victims."[2]

Dr. Baruch Goldstein, who massacred Muslims in the Hebron incident, is described by Juergensmeyer as being motivated by intense feelings of humiliation and fear when he heard Palestinian youths shouting "*itbah al-yahud*," which means "slaughter the Jews."[3] In the background of the Israeli consciousness is the memory of the Holocaust, when Germans were shouting the exact same thing. It is notable that both Rantisi and Goldstein were medical doctors, trained to heal human sicknesses. But the kind of education that is needed to heal spiritual and political sickness is not a part of the curriculum of any medical school that I am aware of.

2. Juergensmeyer, *Terror in the Mind of God*, 74.

3. Ibid., 49–52.

In our survey of examples of hypocrisy, we may consider also the "War on Terrorism" carried out by the United States government in the wake of the 9/11 attacks. President Bush speaks of "evildoers" who must be "brought to justice."[4] Even without criticizing the clumsy self-righteousness of this language, at the very least we must admit that the prosecution of this war has led to the deaths of innocent civilians in Afghanistan and Iraq, so that those who conduct the war would have to admit their participation in the fallenness and guilt of human existence. They could only remain blind to the truth that hypocrisy is the human condition by insisting that since their motivations are pure and noble in their own minds they are exempt from any guilt whatsoever. The indefensibility of such an attitude is obvious enough that it needs no refutation.

To shift gears slightly, consider the way presidential (and congressional) campaigns are conducted in the United States (and there is no reason to think that campaigns conducted elsewhere are any different). The rhetoric of these campaigns (seen most clearly in the television ads) is a strange mixture of sentimentality and brutality. That is, the ads paint a rosy, sentimental picture of the favored candidate, and a lurid, biased, brutal picture of the opposing candidate. The motivations and character of one candidate are above reproach, and the motivations and character of the other are so hateful that they really ought to be incarcerated rather than elected. I have found a quotation that expresses this situation eloquently:

> The leaders of one party meet here and nominate a man, and the leaders of another party meet there, and nominate another candidate, and a third person gets upon a stump and nominates himself, and then they all go to work, and make their respective presses groan under the misrepresentations, slanders and falsehoods, with which they assail each other until the day of voting, when one of them is elected, and is thereby constituted a law maker.[5]

This was written in 1846 by Luther Lee, an abolitionist minister. How little things have changed since then is a perfect example of my

4. For an amplification of this point, see Lincoln, "Symmetric Dualisms: Bush and bin Laden on October 7," chap. 2 in *Holy Terrors*.

5. Lee, *Five Sermons and a Tract by Luther Lee*, 52.

contention that hypocrisy is the human condition.[6] Candidates cannot imagine any other way of conducting themselves than to accuse the other of wrongdoing while conveniently forgetting their own fallibility.

Speaking more broadly regarding the "culture wars" that are such a prominent feature of the contemporary world, my portrayal of the human condition is amplified once again. Whenever "liberals" face off against "conservatives" the accusations fly through the air with a perfect sense of self-righteousness.[7] It is always *the others* who are in the wrong, never oneself or one's own ideological camp.[8] Whether the issue is abortion, sexual ethics, the environment, the teaching of evolution, or whatever else is the topic of the day, it makes no difference concerning the self-righteous attitudes of the participants and the good us vs. evil them structure of the arguments. René Girard makes this comment:

> Duping oneself is what characterizes the entire satanic process, and that is why one of the titles of the devil is "prince of darkness." In revealing the self-deception of those who engage in violence, the New Testament dispels the lie at the heart of their violence. It spells out everything we need to reject our own mythic view of ourselves, our belief in our own innocence. (ISS, 127)

The flip side of the myth of the victim's guilt is the innocence of those who are killing the victim.

The practice of capital punishment in the United States is another key example of hypocrisy in action. Violent criminals often take the process of mimetic desire to an absurd and pathological extreme, and at that point society says that they must be executed. But society cannot admit that it is working according to the same principle of mimetic

6. Recall the 2004 presidential campaign between George Bush, John Kerry, and Ralph Nader, who nominated himself. The Eliot Spitzer prostitution scandal occurred during the final revisions of this book. The hypocrisy aspect of it is rather obvious, but I need to reemphasize that my main thesis in this chapter is not that *some* people are hypocritical, but that we all are. Some situations are merely more dramatic than others.

7. See Hunter, *Culture Wars*, and "The Discourse of Negation and the Ironies of Common Culture."

8. See Mathewes, "Christian Intellectuals and Escapism after 9/11." This essay is an extremely insightful critique of the hypocrisy involved in left-wing reactions to 9/11. "Today the left does not worry about who its friends are, because it's too busy hating its enemies" (307).

desire at a lower dosage. It is as if ten tons of low-grade radioactive uranium is saying to a pound of enriched uranium "You're bad!" "You're evil!" The death penalty can only be carried out in a society that has rejected the meaning of the story of the woman caught in adultery, a society that is too blind to see its own hypocrisy.

If we look at history the number of examples of hypocrisy we can point to multiplies exponentially. Think of Luther's diatribe against the "murdering, robbing, hordes of peasants" who must be slain and sent to hell just as you would kill a mad dog. Here is the apostle of God's grace speaking with the voice of hypocrisy at a fevered pitch that has hardly ever been equaled. Or consider the medieval Crusaders who slew "the infidels" in the name of Christ, the Prince of Peace. When we think of the critics of Christianity, such as Marx and Nietzsche, what is it that they most commonly accuse Christians of? Hypocrisy. Christians are concerned with straining out the gnats of petty personal sins while swallowing a camel by enjoying the fruits of an exploitative economic system that grinds the poor into the grave. Or Christians present themselves as the champions of "good" that is able to critique "evil," even as they are motivated by suppressed hatred and desires for revenge against their true superiors. When those who read Marx and Nietzsche and were inspired by them to great deeds walked to and fro upon the earth in the twentieth century, what did they do? They sought to make the world a better place, of course. And how did they do this? The Marxists set out to improve society by killing millions of people. The ferocity with which means were separated from ends in their thinking is truly impressive. The unspoken presupposition of this movement is aptly described by Reinhold Niebuhr: "The Marxist detection of ideological taint in the thought of all bourgeois culture is significantly unembarrassed by any scruples about the conditioned character of its own viewpoints."[9] The Nazis claimed to be doing the world a favor by ridding it of all "Jewish vermin." In the process, the Nazis brought so much evil into the world that if it could be measured somehow it would vastly exceed the measure of even their own insane accusations against the Jews. In other words, the Marxists and the Nazis "made the world a better place" by committing acts of hypocritical barbarity and mass killing that were without equal in world history.

9. Niebuhr, *Nature and Destiny of Man*, 1:201.

The United States government dropped bombs that killed hundreds of thousands of civilians during World War II, rejecting one the basic tenets of the Just War Theory, non-combatant immunity.[10] After the war, the victors put Axis leaders on trial as war criminals. But have victors *ever* in human history put *themselves* on trial for their own decisions that resulted in the deaths of civilians? The idea is unthinkable, of course. That unthinkability proves my thesis.

I rest my case. *Hypocrisy is the human condition. It is the most basic anthropological feature of human beings in their fallen state, to accuse others of doing wrong when they themselves are doing wrong.*

"The victims most interesting to us are always those who allow us to condemn our neighbors. And our neighbors do the same . . ." says René Girard (ISS, 164). His thought, at its heart, is a brilliant exposé of hypocrisy as the human condition. He has shown that human culture is formed and maintained around acts of scapegoating. Society points its finger at someone it has chosen to vent its frustration upon. The victim is blamed for the society's ills. "You are guilty! You are evil! We will do away with you!" are chanted in preparation for the act of violence. Of course, society refuses to see that the act of scapegoating itself is immoral; it takes wisdom from outside the social system to realize that scapegoating demonstrates the essentially unethical character of human life when it is dominated by mimetic desire. Girard shows us that the crowd is doing something wrong in the act of accusing the victim of doing something wrong. One of the Bible's key accomplishments is the unveiling of structural social hypocrisy as the most deadly aspect of human sinfulness. The ministry of Jesus is the clearest working out of this prophetic revelation of the structure of human sin.

Consider this passage of sacred literature that is at the root of the Abrahamic religions: The Serpent said to Adam and Eve, "You will not die; for God knows that when you eat of it your eyes will be opened, and you will be like God, knowing good and evil" (Gen 3:5). To fall into sin is to presume that we are justified in thinking of ourselves as good and someone else as evil. Karl Barth expresses this idea forcefully:

10. See Carter, *Rethinking Christ and Culture*, 131–34. Talal Asad's *On Suicide Bombing* contains thoughtful reflections on the double-standards that are often at work in Western political ethics.

> The truth is that when man thinks that he can hold the front against the devil in his own strength and by his own invention and intention, the devil has already gained his point. And he [the devil] looks triumphantly over his [man's] shoulder from behind, for man has now become a great fighter in his cause. I am already choosing wrong when I think that I know and ought to decide what is right, and I am doing wrong when I try to accomplish that which I have chosen as right. I am already putting myself in the wrong with others, and doing them wrong, when—it makes no odds how gently or vigorously I do it—I confront them as the one who is right, wanting to break over them as the great crisis. For when I do this I divide myself and I break the fellowship between myself and others. I can only live at unity with myself, and we can only live in fellowship with one another, when I and we subject ourselves to the right which does not dwell in us and is not manifested by us, but which is over me and us as the right of God above.[11]

Hypocrisy is the epistemology, the way of knowing, that is Satan's gift to us. We love this gift. We treasure it more highly than anything else in this world. It gives us energy and a sense of purpose in life. It enables us to break out of the vise in which we find ourselves and go forth into the world as decisive actors who are "like God," doing God's will. In other words, eating the fruit can just as accurately be described as the fall into righteousness as the fall into sin. The two concepts are convertible.

President George W. Bush is the paradigmatic human being. He is Adam for our moment in time. He represents all of us, in that we are all self-righteous, "knowing good and evil." If someone is reading these words and thinking to him or herself, "those Republicans sure are fallen; I'm glad we Democrats aren't," then I am a complete failure in my attempts to communicate an idea. (Either that or the reader is a complete failure as a reader.) To know good and evil comes with the political office; it does not matter who resides in the office or what their party affiliation is. Democratic presidents dropped the bomb on Hiroshima, went to war in Vietnam, and did nothing while Cain slaughtered his brothers and sisters in Rwanda.

11. Barth, *Church Dogmatics*, IV/1:451.

I spoke above concerning two unrealistic attempts to avoid the uncomfortable insight that hypocrisy is the human condition: to be sinless or to decide not to judge anyone, ever, for any reason. There is a third possibility that is not quite an escape from the human condition, but at least it is an attitude that I find to be somewhat more commendable and hopeful for the future than is unselfconscious hypocrisy. One can point to forgiveness and grace. From a Jewish perspective, Jonathan Sacks makes this point powerfully:

> [Forgiveness] answers hate with a refusal to hate, animosity with generosity. Few more daring ideas have ever entered the human situation. Forgiveness means that we are not destined endlessly to replay the grievances of yesterday. It is the ability the live with the past without being held captive by the past. It would not be an exaggeration to say that forgiveness is the most compelling testimony to human freedom. It is about the action that is not reaction. It is the refusal to be defined by circumstance. It represents our ability to change course, reframe the narrative of the past and create an unexpected set of possibilities for the future.[12]

Charles Taylor makes an almost identical argument:

> The higher the morality, the more vicious the hatred and hence destruction we can, indeed must, wreak. When the crusade comes to its fullness in the moralism of the modern world, even the last vestiges of chivalric respect for an enemy, as in the days of Saladin and Richard Coeur de Lion, have disappeared. There is nothing left but the grim, relentless struggle against evil.
>
> There is no general remedy against this self-righteous reconstitution of the categorizations of violence, the lines drawn between the good and evil ones that permit the most terrible atrocities. But there can be moves, always within a given context, whereby someone renounces the right conferred by suffering, the right of the innocent to punish the guilty, of the victim to purge the victimizer. The move is the very opposite of the instinctive defense of our righteousness. It is a move that can be called forgiveness, but at a deeper level, it is based on a recognition of common, flawed humanity.[13]

12. Sacks, *Dignity of Difference*, 179.

13. Taylor, "Notes on the Sources of Violence," 39. See also Jozef Niewiadomski's

Christianity, at its worst, is simply another form of hypocrisy. But at its best, it is a way of existing as a human being that embodies humility in relationship with God (rather than arrogant self-righteousness and idolatry), openness to growth in selfhood (rather than egocentric refusal to change), and social solidarity (rather than splitting the world into 'good' and 'evil' camps). When Christianity points to God's grace in its liturgy, its teaching, and its practices in the world, it becomes one of those very rare places where a genuine alternative to hypocrisy is found. This is why the saying "I don't go to church because it's full of hypocrites" is so short-sighted.

A Prayer

Just and merciful God, whose glory fills the whole creation, open our eyes to your goodness and truth; draw our hearts to you as we walk through this world; replace our anxiety and fear with faith in you. Lord Jesus Christ, light of the world, reveal to us the glory of the Father; draw us forward into the path of grace; teach us to offer to others the forgiveness we have received from you; lift our hearts with the hope that comes from above. Holy Spirit, giver of life, teach us to treasure the lives of our neighbors, just as we treasure our own; remind us always that it is right, and a good and joyful thing, to give thanks to God for the gift of love. Holy Trinity, source of all things, seen and unseen, form us in your image; fill us with your joy; draw us to your eternal light even now, as we walk through the darkness of this world that has forgotten and abandoned you. Amen.

excellent essay on apocalyptic thinking. "Without God's interference, humans would mutually condemn one another to the hell of accusation, denial, and lies. Everyone would insist on victim status, demand retribution, and pass the retribution facing him or her on to others." Niewiadomski, "Denial of the Apocalypse," 65.

9

Conclusion

§ WHEN *THE TIMES* ASKED SEVERAL LEADING INTELLECTUALS TO REFLECT on "what is wrong with the world," G. K. Chesterton submitted a letter that simply read: "I am." That was his way of reminding us that if we seek to understand the corruption of human beings, we must look inward; we must develop self-knowledge. But one of the surest observations that we can make about human beings is that they fear self-knowledge more than anything else—more even than death. This book has been an attempt to deal hammer blows to our lack of self-knowledge. Perhaps that is the wrong approach. Can self-knowledge be beaten into peoples' heads? Perhaps self-knowledge ought to be drawn out through gentle leading and persuasion. I have done what I know how to do; I will let the chips fall where they may.[1]

§ The basic problem with the human race is that we would rather kill than think; if we were to take thinking seriously, we would have to change, and we do not want to change. This is my thesis in the smallest possible nutshell.

§ In the third part of the book, there is a dialectic at work. I begin with an analysis of the pathology of the 9/11 hijackers. It is easy to think of them as "external" to ourselves. The next chapter, which rewrites a presidential speech, brings the issues closer to home. The reader who takes the time to compare what I have written with the speech that was actually given will understand my implied critique. It is not simply the case that President Bush has fallen into the vortex of mimicking violence; he represents all of us, to the extent that we want to be in that vortex

1. For further reflections on human fear of self-knowledge, see Alasdair MacIntyre's essay, "What Has Christianity to Say to the Moral Philosopher?"

of our own free will. The chapter on hypocrisy completes the dialectic by bringing the analysis all the way home. The tendency to justify in one's own mind verbal or literal violence toward others is the human condition. As I was writing this, I had two quotations in the back of my mind:

> The Master said, "When walking with two other people, I will always find a teacher among them. Those who are good I seek to emulate, and those who are bad provide me with reminders of what I need to change in myself."[2]

> *Homo sum, humani nil a me alienum puto.* [I am a man, nothing human is alien to me.][3]

If we look at the "evildoers" such as the 9/11 hijackers, and simply view them as monsters, external to ourselves, then we are rejecting an absolutely crucial insight—namely, that when we comprehend the roots of violence we are looking into our own souls. We are engaging in self-examination.

My rhetorical strategy is a version of Kierkegaard's notion of "thoughts which wound from behind": "The essentially Christian needs no *defense*, is not served by any *defense*—it is the *attacker*; to defend it is of all perversions the most indefensible, the most *inverted*, and the most dangerous—it is *unconsciously cunning treason*. Christianity is the attacker—in Christendom, of course, it attacks from behind" (CD, 162). Because Christendom is actually based on a rejection of the central insights of the Gospel, those insights sneak up behind us to remind us how far we are from actually understanding what it means to follow Christ. The only way that human beings can actually change is when we agree with certain ideas that are presented to us, not realizing that what we have agreed to is actually a seed that has been planted in us that will eventually undo our current way of thinking. Whether or not this strategy is successful depends upon how this book is received.

§ At the heart of my argument in this book there is a vision of moral geometry.[4] The dimensions of reality and how they intersect is a geo-

2. *Annalects of Confucius* 7:21.

3. Terence, *Heauton Timoroumenos*, line 77.

4. I am indebted to Pierre Manent for this phrase. See *The City of Man*, 202. In that chapter, Manent describes the moral geometry of the modern soul as it seeks to flee

metrical concept. In another sense, my argument can be seen as creating a fractal image, which is characterized by self-similarity.[5] In other words, one begins by looking at a particular shape; one then zooms in to see greater detail; one zooms in again and again, noticing that the original shape that one saw appears over and over at different levels, which allows the zooming in process to continue infinitely. I have argued that dimensional complexity has its origin in the character of the triune God; when we look carefully at our world we see the dimensional vectors refracted in human thought and behavior patterns, in the emphases of thinkers, in the components of theological method, in time as cosmic, psychological, and cultural, in love of God, self, and neighbor, and so forth.[6] That we can see the same pattern in the three faces of Satan and in the roots of violence makes sense in connection with the idea that Satan has no originality; he is the eternal fraud who apes after God and seeks to ruin God's creation.

§ A black hole cannot be observed with telescopes because light cannot escape from it, but its existence can be inferred from the behavior of other nearby objects in space. This is a rough analogy for my linkage of anthropological analysis and the Trinity. God cannot be observed

---

from both divine grace (as articulated by the Christian tradition) and nature (as articulated by Greek philosophy), by creating for itself History as the realm of autonomous individual freedom. In terms of my analysis, he is describing a refusal to live in the vertical dimension, leading to a narrow focus on selfhood. His argument unveils the incoherencies that are entailed by this refusal to inhabit complexity. "In his immaturity, man lived between two worlds and at times he thought there was one too many. Thanks to the labors of modern philosophy, he has arrived at autonomy and banished the other world, but he has lost this one" (198).

5. My knowledge of Hegel's thought is very limited and sketchy, in that my attempts to read him led to frustration at his impenetrable prose. I am aware that there are triadic elements in his thought that are similar to this fractal image concept. Samuel Powell argues that the twentieth-century revival of Trinitarian theology has been deeply influenced by Hegel (Powell, *The Trinity in German Thought*, 141). In that my argument seeks to continue this revival, there is a connection between Hegel's thought and mine, but I do not have anything further to say on that topic beyond noting that it is not a direct influence.

6. H. Richard Niebuhr had a similar intuition: "God's love of self and neighbor, neighbor's love of God and self, and self's love of God and neighbor are so closely interrelated that none of the relations exists without the others. The intricacy and unity of the human situation before God is not less dynamic and complex than the one we encounter in nature when we explore the energetic world of the atom or of a sidereal [astronomical] system." *The Purpose of the Church and Its Ministry*, 34.

directly, but God's existence and character can be seen in the negative shadows projected by human rebellion against the triune God.

Human beings have the ability to rebel against God in ways that the lower animals cannot. This brings to mind two quotations: first, ". . . not even lions or dragons have ever waged such wars among themselves as men have" (Augustine), and second, ". . . man is the only wild animal" (Chesterton).[7] In the terms we have developed in this book, human beings are the only animals who can refuse to live within the structure of reality—warping it, unbalancing it, twisting it, and using the energy of their twisting motions to slaughter each other in massive numbers.

Imagine one of those pictures that has a fuzzy set of lines that seems to represent nothing in particular, but if you stare at it long enough your brain finally sees an image of a waterfall or a unicorn. This process might be helped by someone coming along side of you and telling you what to look for. My goal in this book is to come alongside the reader for whom the chaos of human history is a fuzzy confusion and point out how the Triune God can actually be seen in it. Once you see the image, your brain will always recognize it. There is no going back. This idea was affirmed by Kierkegaard, Voegelin, and Girard, each in his own way. Christianity has impacted the world in decisive ways, and there is no going back.

§ Theologians speak about the relationship between *law* and *gospel*. The *law* that comes down from above convicts us of our sin; the *gospel* brings us grace and forgiveness. We live in a world in which human beings have arrogated to themselves the function of law and have rejected the gospel. We can see this clearly in the 9/11 hijackers, who thought of themselves as divinely inspired executioners, crushing the sinful world of Westerners with the weight of *Islamic law* (in their twisted interpretation of it). But I was also implying in my "Speech Not Given" that there was a similar response from the Bush administration; it saw itself as having the duty to crush the "evildoers" with the weight of *American imperial law*. To think of oneself as the judge of the world without recognizing fully that one is also under judgment is the essence of hypocrisy. What the world needs most is not more *law*; we need the gospel, lived out in actions. In neither set of actors (hijackers / Bush) has the gospel been clearly heard so that it becomes the central principle

7. Augustine *City of God* 12.23 (Dyson, 534); Chesterton, *Orthodoxy*, chap. 9.

of action. We see a "clash of fundamentalisms," but we do not see the pathway that leads to a different, healthier, more ethical future for the human race.

When people climb out on a limb and live an unbalanced life that overemphasizes one of the dimensions at the expense of the others, the result is the blindness that leads to hypocrisy. The light shines from the Center; climbing out on a limb means moving into the dark shadowlands. Living in the Center, which is constituted by the gospel Christ preaches, is the only pathway to truly *seeing* reality. If a scientist is one who sees clearly by disentangling his or her vision from the foggy confusions of unreflective human culture, then Christ is the ultimate scientist of the spirit. Thinkers such as Kierkegaard, Voegelin, and Girard are walking in his footsteps, giving us glimpses, as they are able, of what they have seen. Some day we will wake up from our blindness and hypocrisy and move toward the Center. This awakening will be the fruit of the breaking into our world of God's grace and truth, that grace and truth that became incarnate two thousand years ago in God's Son.

Bibliography

Abdul Rauf, Feisal. *What's Right with Islam: A New Vision for Muslims and the West.* San Francisco: HarperSanFrancisco, 2004.

Abou El Fadl, Khaled. *The Great Theft: Wrestling Islam from the Extremists.* New York: HarperSanFrancisco, 2007.

Alison, James. *Faith Beyond Resentment: Fragments Catholic and Gay.* New York: Crossroad, 2001.

Asad, Talal. *On Suicide Bombing.* New York: Columbia University Press, 2007.

Augustine, *Augustine: Later Works.* Edited by John Burnaby. Philadelphia: Westminster, 1955.

———. *The City of God against the Pagans.* Translated by R. W. Dyson. New York: Cambridge University Press, 1998.

Aulen, Gustav. *Christus Victor: An Historical Study of the Three Main Types of Atonement.* New York: Macmillan, 1931.

Bailie, Gil. *Violence Unveiled: Humanity at the Crossroads.* New York: Crossroad, 1995.

Barth, Karl. *Christ and Adam: Man and Humanity in Romans 5.* Translated by T. A. Smail. New York: Macmillan, 1956.

———. *The Christian Life.* Translated by G. W. Bromiley. Grand Rapids: Eerdmans, 1981.

———. *Church Dogmatics.* Edited by G. W. Bromiley and T. F. Torrance. Edinburgh: T & T Clark, 1956–69.

———. *The Epistle to the Romans.* Translated by Edwyn C. Hoskyns. London: Oxford University Press, 1968.

———. *God Here and Now.* Translated by Paul M. van Buren. New York: Harper & Row, 1964.

Bauman, Zygmunt. *Modernity and the Holocaust.* Ithaca, NY: Cornell University Press, 1989.

Bellinger, Charles K. "Abortion and the Struggle against Tyranny in American History." MA Thesis. University of Virginia, 1992.

———. "'The Crowd is Untruth': A Comparison of Kierkegaard and Girard." *Contagion: A Journal of Violence, Mimesis, and Culture* 3 (1996) 103–19.

———. *The Genealogy of Violence: Reflections on Creation, Freedom, and Evil.* New York: Oxford University Press, 2001.

———. "Kierkegaard's *Either/Or* and the Parable of the Prodigal Son: Or, Three Rival Versions of Three Rival Versions." In *International Kierkegaard Commentary: Either/Or,* Part II, edited by Robert L. Perkins, 59–82. Macon, GA: Mercer University Press, 1995.

———. "Toward a Kierkegaardian Understanding of Hitler, Stalin, and the Cold War." In *Foundations of Kierkegaard's Vision of Community: Religion, Ethics, and*

Politics in Kierkegaard, edited by George Connell and C. Stephen Evans, 218–30. Atlantic Highlands, NJ: Humanities, 1992.

———. "Understanding Violence: The New Copernican Revolution." In *The Just War and Jihad: Violence in Judaism, Christianity, and Islam*, edited by R. Joseph Hoffmann, 63–76. Amherst, NY: Prometheus, 2006.

Berdyaev, Nikolai. *Slavery and Freedom*. Translated by R. M. French. New York: Scribners, 1944.

Bonhoeffer, Dietrich. *Christ the Center*. Translated by John Bowden. New York: Harper & Row, 1966.

Brooks, Phillips. *Phillips Brooks: Selected Sermons*. Edited by William Scarlett. New York: Dutton, 1950.

Cady, Linell E. *Religion, Theology, and American Public Life*. Albany: State University of New York Press, 1993.

Cahill, Lisa Sowle. *Love Your Enemies: Discipleship, Pacifism, and Just War Theory*. Minneapolis: Fortress, 1994.

Callahan, Sidney Cornelia. "Abortion and the Sexual Agenda: A Case for Prolife Feminism." In *Abortion: A Reader*, edited by Lloyd Steffen, 340–53. Cleveland: Pilgrim, 1996.

———. *With All Our Heart and Mind: The Spiritual Works of Mercy in a Psychological Age*. New York: Crossroad, 1988.

Carter, Craig A. *Rethinking Christ and Culture: A Post-Christendom Perspective*. Grand Rapids: Brazos, 2006.

Cary, Phillip. *Augustine's Invention of the Inner Self: The Legacy of a Christian Platonist*. New York: Oxford University Press, 2000.

Cavanaugh, William T. *Theopolitical Imagination*. New York: T. & T. Clark, 2002.

Chesterton, G. K. *Orthodoxy*. New York: Dodd, Mead, 1924.

Clément, Olivier. *On Human Being: A Spiritual Anthropology*. Translated by Jeremy Hummerstone. New York: New City Press, 2000.

Cooper, Barry. *New Political Religions, Or, An Analysis of Modern Terrorism*. Eric Voegelin Institute Series in Political Philosophy: Columbia: University of Missouri Press, 2004.

Cooper, Terry. *Dimensions of Evil: Contemporary Perspectives*. Minneapolis: Fortress Press, 2007.

Cunningham, David S. *These Three Are One: The Practice of Trinitarian Theology*. Malden, MA: Blackwell, 1998.

Edwards, Jonathan. *The Nature of True Virtue*. Eugene, OR: Wipf & Stock, 2003.

Eliot, T. S. *The Sacred Wood: Essays on Poetry and Criticism*. 6th ed. London: Methuen, 1948.

Eller, Vernard. *Kierkegaard and Radical Discipleship: A New Perspective*. Princeton: Princeton University Press, 1968.

Ellul, Jacques. *The New Demons*. Translated by C. Edward Hopkin. New York: Seabury, 1975.

Erickson, Millard. *Christian Theology*. 2nd ed. Grand Rapids: Baker, 1998.

Evans, C. Stephen. *Søren Kierkegaard's Christian Psychology*. Grand Rapids: Zondervan, 1990.

Federici, Michael. *Eric Voegelin: The Restoration of Order*. Wilmington, DL: ISI, 2002.

Ferreira, M. Jamie. *Love's Grateful Striving: A Commentary on Kierkegaard's Works of Love*. New York: Oxford University Press, 2001.

Fodor, Jim. "Christian Discipleship as Participative Imitation: Theological Reflections on Girardian Themes." In *Violence Renounced: René Girard, Biblical Studies, and Peacemaking*, edited by Willard M. Swartley, 246–76. Telford, PA: Pandora, 2000.

Gorringe, Timothy. *God's Just Vengeance: Crime, Violence and the Rhetoric of Salvation*. New York: Cambridge University Press, 1996.

Gourevitch, Philip. *We Wish to Inform You That Tomorrow We Will Be Killed with Our Families: Stories from Rwanda*. New York: Farrar, Straus and Giroux, 1998.

Gouwens, David J. *Kierkegaard as Religious Thinker*. Cambridge: Cambridge University Press, 1996.

Grant, Edward. *Physical Science in the Middle Ages*. New York: Wiley, 1971.

Grant, George Parkin. *English-Speaking Justice*. Notre Dame: University of Notre Dame Press, 1985.

Grøn, Arne. "The Human Synthesis." In *Anthropology and Authority: Essays on Søren Kierkegaard*, edited by Poul Houe, Gordon D. Marino, and Sven Hakon Rossel, 27–32. Amsterdam: Rodopi, 2000.

Gunton, Colin E. *Intellect and Action: Elucidations on Christian Theology and the Life of Faith*. Edinburgh: T. & T. Clark, 2000.

Gushee, David P. *Only Human: Christian Reflections on the Journey Toward Wholeness*. San Francisco: Jossey-Bass, 2005.

Harris, Sam. *The End of Faith: Religion, Terror, and the Future of Reason*. New York: Norton, 2004.

Hart, David Bentley. *The Beauty of the Infinite: The Aesthetics of Christian Truth*. Grand Rapids: Eerdmans, 2003.

———. "Daniel Dennett Hunts the Snark." *First Things* 169 (2007) 30–38.

———. *The Doors of the Sea: Where Was God in the Tsunami?* Grand Rapids: Eerdmans, 2005.

———. "God or Nothingness." In *I Am the Lord Your God: Christian Reflections on the Ten Commandments*, edited by Carl E. Braaten and Christopher R. Seitz, 55–76. Grand Rapids: Eerdmans, 2005.

Hauerwas, Stanley M. *Christian Existence Today: Essays on Church, World, and Living In Between*. 1988. Reprint, Grand Rapids: Brazos, 2001.

Heilke, Thomas W. *Eric Voegelin: In Quest of Reality*. Lanham, MD: Rowman & Littlefield, 1999.

Heim, S. Mark. *The Depth of the Riches: A Trinitarian Theology of Religious Ends*. Grand Rapids: Eerdmans, 2001.

———. *Saved from Sacrifice: A Theology of the Cross*. Grand Rapids: Eerdmans, 2006.

Hughes, Glenn. "Balanced and Unbalanced Consciousness." In *The Politics of the Soul: Eric Voegelin on Religious Experience*, edited by Glenn Hughes, 163–83. Lanham, MD: Rowman & Littlefield, 1999.

———. *Transcendence and History*. Columbia: University of Missouri Press, 2003.

Hunsinger, George. *Disruptive Grace: Studies in the Theology of Karl Barth*. Grand Rapids: Eerdmans, 2000.

Hunter, James Davison. *Culture Wars: The Struggle to Define America*. New York: Basic, 1991.

———. "The Discourse of Negation and the Ironies of Common Culture." *The Hedgehog Review* 6.3 (2004) 24–38.

Ignatieff, Michael. *The Warrior's Honor: Ethnic War and the Modern Conscience*. New York: Holt, 1997.

Illich, Ivan, and David Cayley. *The Rivers North of the Future: The Testament of Ivan Illich*. Toronto: Anansi, 2005.

Jenson, Robert. *On Thinking the Human: Resolutions of Difficult Notions*. Grand Rapids: Eerdmans, 2003.

———. *Systematic Theology: Volume I: The Triune God*. New York: Oxford University Press, 1997.

Johnson, Eric L. *Foundations for Soul Care: A Christian Psychology Proposal*. Downers Grove, IL: InterVarsity, 2007.

Juergensmeyer, Mark. *Terror in the Mind of God: The Global Rise of Religious Violence*. Berkeley: University of California Press, 2000.

Kant, Immanuel. *The Conflict of the Faculties*. Translated by Mary J. Gregor. Lincoln, NB: University of Nebraska Press, 1979.

Kimball, Charles. *When Religion Becomes Evil*. San Francisco: HarperSanFrancisco, 2002.

King, Martin Luther, Jr. "The Three Dimensions of a Complete Life." In *A Knock at Midnight: Inspiration from the Great Sermons of Reverend Martin Luther King, Jr.*, edited by Clayborne Carson and Peter Holloran, 117–40. New York: Warner, 1998.

Kirmmse, Bruce H. *Kierkegaard in Golden-Age Denmark*. Bloomington: Indiana University Press, 1990.

———, editor. *Encounters with Kierkegaard: A Life as Seen by His Contemporaries*. Princeton: Princeton University Press, 1996.

Koenigsberg, Richard. "The Sacrificial Meaning of the Holocaust." No pages. Online: http://home.earthlink.net/~libraryofsocialscience/sacrificial_meaning.htm.

Lee, Luther. *Five Sermons and a Tract by Luther Lee*. Edited by Donald W. Dayton. Chicago: Holrad, 1975.

Lenin, Vladimir. *The Lenin Anthology*. Edited by Robert C. Tucker. New York: Norton, 1975.

Lincoln, Bruce. *Holy Terrors: Thinking about Religion after September 11*. Chicago: University of Chicago Press, 2003.

MacArthur, John. *Terrorism, Jihad, and the Bible: A Response to the Terrorist Attacks*. Nashville: W Publishing Group, 2001.

MacIntyre, Alasdair. *After Virtue: A Study in Moral Theory*. 2nd ed. Notre Dame: University of Notre Dame Press, 1984.

———. *Three Rival Versions of Moral Enquiry: Encyclopaedia, Genealogy, and Tradition*. Notre Dame: University of Notre Dame Press, 1990.

———. "What Has Christianity to Say to the Moral Philosopher?" In *The Doctrine of God and Theological Ethics*, edited by Alan J. Torrance and Michael Banner, 17–32. New York: T. & T. Clark, 2006.

Malantschuk, Gregor. *Kierkegaard's Thought*. Translated by Howard V. Hong and Edna H. Hong. Princeton: Princeton University Press, 1971.

Manent, Pierre. *The City of Man*. Translated by Marc A. LePain. Princeton: Princeton University Press, 1998.

Marx, Karl, and Friedrich Engels. *The Marx-Engels Reader*. Edited by Robert C. Tucker. New York: Norton, 1978.

Mathewes, Charles T. "Christian Intellectuals and Escapism after 9/11." In *Strike Terror No More: Theology, Ethics, and the New War*, edited by Jon L. Berquist, 306–15. St. Louis, MO: Chalice, 2002.

McBride, James. "Capital Punishment as the Unconstitutional Establishment of Religion: A Girardian Reading of the Death Penalty." *Journal of Church and State* 37 (1995) 263–87.

McKinnon, Alastair. "Kierkegaard and the 'Leap of Faith.'" *Kierkegaardiana* 16 (1993) 107–25.

Meddeb, Abdelwahab. *The Malady of Islam*. Translated by Pierre Joris and Ann Reid. New York: Basic, 2003.

Moltmann, Jürgen. "Hope and History." *Theology Today* 25 (1968) 369–86.

Neiman, Susan. *Evil in Modern Thought: An Alternative History of Philosophy*. Princeton: Princeton University Press, 2002.

Neuhaus, Richard John. "The Religion of the Sovereign Self." In *The Right Choice*, edited by Paul T. Stallsworth, 61–68. Nashville: Abingdon, 1997.

Newman, John Henry. "The Three Offices of Christ." No pages. Online: http://www.newmanreader.org/works/subjects/sermon5.html.

Niebuhr, H. Richard. *Christ and Culture*. New York: HarperCollins, 2001.

———. "The Doctrine of the Trinity and the Unity of the Church." *Theology Today* 3 (1946) 371–84. Reprinted as "Theological Unitarianisms." *Theology Today* 40 (July 1983) 150–56. http://theologytoday.ptsem.edu/jul1983/v40-2-article3.htm.

———. *The Purpose of the Church and Its Ministry*. New York: Harper & Row, 1956.

———. *The Responsible Self*. New York: Harper & Row, 1963.

———. *Theology, History, and Culture: Major Unpublished Writings*. Edited by William Stacy Johnson. New Haven: Yale University Press, 1996.

Niebuhr, Reinhold. *An Interpretation of Christian Ethics*. New York: Meridian, 1956.

———. *The Nature and Destiny of Man*. New York: Scribners, 1941.

———. *Reinhold Niebuhr on Politics: His Political Philosophy and Its Application to Our Age as Expressed in His Writings*. Edited by Harry R. Davis and Robert C. Good. New York: Scribners, 1960.

Nietzsche, Friedrich. *The Will to Power*. Edited by Walter Kaufmann. New York: Vintage Books, 1967.

Niewiadomski, Jozef. "'Denial of the Apocalypse' versus 'Fascination with the Final Days': Current Theological Discussion of Apocalyptic Thinking in the Perspective of Mimetic Theory." In *Politics & Apocalypse*, edited by Robert Hamerton-Kelly, 51–68. Studies in Violence, Mimesis, and Culture. East Lansing: Michigan State University Press, 2007.

Nyssa, Gregory of, St. *Gregory of Nyssa's Treatise on the Inscriptions of the Psalms*. Translated by Ronald E. Heine. New York: Oxford University Press, 1995.

Ortega y Gasset, José. *The Revolt of the Masses*. New York: Norton, 1957.

Percy, Walker. *Signposts in a Strange Land*. Edited by Patrick Samway. New York: Farrar, Straus, and Giroux, 1991.

Pinckaers, Servais. *Morality: The Catholic View*. Translated by Michael Sherwin. South Bend, IN: St. Augustine's, 2001.

———. *The Sources of Christian Ethics*. Translated by Mary Thomas Noble. Washington, DC: Catholic University of America Press, 1995.

Powell, Samuel M. *The Trinity in German Thought*. New York: Cambridge University Press, 2001.

Ramsey, Michael. *God, Christ, and the World: A Study in Contemporary Theology*. New York: Morehouse–Barlow, 1969.

Ranieri, John. "What Voegelin Missed in the Gospel." *Contagion* 7 (2000) 125–59.

Reno, R. R. *In the Ruins of the Church: Sustaining Faith in an Age of Diminished Christianity*. Grand Rapids: Brazos, 2002.

———. *Redemptive Change: Atonement and the Christian Cure of the Soul*. Harrisburg, PA: Trinity, 2002.

———. "Stanley Hauerwas." In *The Blackwell Companion to Political Theology*, edited by William T. Cavanaugh and Peter Scott, 302–16. Malden, MA: Blackwell, 2004.

Russell, Jeffrey Burton. *Inventing the Flat Earth: Columbus and Modern Historians*. New York: Praeger, 1991.

Sacks, Jonathan. *The Dignity of Difference: How to Avoid the Clash of Civilizations*. 2nd ed. New York: Continuum, 2003.

Sandoz, Ellis. *The Voegelinian Revolution*. Baton Rouge: Louisiana State University Press, 1981.

Schmemann, Alexander. *For the Life of the World*. Crestwood, NY: St. Vladimir's Seminary Press, 1973.

Schwager, Raymund. *Banished from Eden: Original Sin and Evolutionary Theory in the Drama of Salvation*. Translated by James Williams. Inigo Text Series 9. Herefordshire, England: Gracewing, 2006.

Sherman, Robert. *King, Priest, and Prophet: A Trinitarian Theology of Atonement*. New York: T. & T. Clark, 2004.

Sherry, Terrence Owen. *The Christo-Morphic Hermeneutical Theology of H. Richard Niebuhr: Shaped by Christ*. Lewiston, NY: Mellen, 2003.

Smail, Thomas A. "In the Image of the Triune God." *International Journal of Systematic Theology* 5 (2003) 22–32.

———. *Like Father, Like Son: The Trinity Imaged in Our Humanity*. Grand Rapids: Eerdmans, 2006.

Stackhouse, Max L. "The Trinity as Public Theology." In *Faith to Creed: Ecumenical Perspectives on the Affirmation of the Apostolic Faith in the Fourth Century*, edited by S. Mark Heim, 162–97. Grand Rapids: Eerdmans, 1991.

Steffen, Lloyd, ed. *Abortion: A Reader*. Cleveland: Pilgrim, 1996.

Stein, Ruth. "Evil as Love and as Liberation." *Psychoanalytic Dialogues* 12.3 (2002) 393–420.

———. "Fundamentalism, Father and Son, and Vertical Desire." *Psychoanalytical Review* 93 (2006) 201–30.

Stern, Jessica. *Terror in the Name of God: Why Religious Militants Kill*. New York: Ecco, 2003.

Swartley, Willard, ed. *Violence Renounced: René Girard, Biblical Studies, and Peacemaking*. Telford, PN: Pandora, 2000.

Swope, Paul. "Abortion: A Failure to Communicate." *First Things* 82 (April 1998) 31–35.

Taylor, Charles. "Notes on the Sources of Violence: Perennial and Modern." In *Beyond Violence: Religious Sources of Social Transformation in Judaism, Christianity, and Islam*, edited by James L. Heft, 15–42. New York: Fordham University Press, 2004.

———. *Sources of the Self: The Making of Modern Identity*. Cambridge: Harvard University Press, 1989.

Tertullian. *Disciplinary, Moral, and Ascetical Works*. Translated by Emily Joseph Daly et al. Fathers of the Church 40. Washington DC: Catholic University of America Press, 1959.

Tinder, Glenn. "Can We Be Good Without God?" *The Atlantic Monthly* (December 1989) 69–85.

———. *The Fabric of Hope: An Essay*. Grand Rapids: Eerdmans, 2001.

———. *The Political Meaning of Christianity: An Interpretation*. Baton Rouge: Louisiana State University Press, 1989.

Torrance, Thomas F. *Theological Science*. New York: Oxford University Press, 1969.

Ward, Bernadette Waterman. "Abortion as a Sacrament: Mimetic Desire and Sacrifice in Sexual Politics." *Contagion* 7 (2000) 18–35.

Westphal, Merold. *Kierkegaard's Critique of Reason and Society*. Macon, GA: Mercer University Press, 1987.

Williams, James G. *The Bible, Violence, and the Sacred: Liberation from the Myth of Sacred Violence*. New York: HarperCollins, 1991.

Yoder, John Howard. *The Politics of Jesus: Vicit Agnus Noster*. 2nd ed. Grand Rapids: Eerdmans, 1994.

———, Glen H. Stassen, and D. M. Yeager. *Authentic Transformation: A New Vision of Christ and Culture*. Nashville: Abingdon, 1996.

Zizioulas, John. *Being as Communion: Studies in Personhood and the Church*. Crestwood, NY: St. Vladimir's Seminary Press, 1997.

Index of Names